LIFE OF CHRIST

BEHOLD THE MAN

AT A GLANCE

Serendipity House / P.O. Box 1012 / Littleton, CO 80160

TOLL FREE 1-800-525-9563 / www.serendipityhouse.com

©1998 Serendipity House. All rights reserved.

99 00 01 02 / **301 series** • **CHG** / 5 4 3 2

PROJECT ENGINEER:
Lyman Coleman

WRITING TEAM:
Richard Peace, Lyman Coleman, Andrew Sloan, Cathy Tardif

PRODUCTION TEAM:
Christopher Werner, Sharon Penington, Erika Tiepel

COVER PHOTO:
© Copyright International by Robert Cushman Hayes, All Rights Reserved

---

CORE VALUES

Community:	The purpose of this curriculum is to build community within the body of believers around Jesus Christ.
Group Process:	To build community, the curriculum must be designed to take a group through a step-by-step process of sharing your story with one another.
Interactive Bible Study:	To share your "story," the approach to Scripture in the curriculum needs to be open-ended and right brain—to "level the playing field" and encourage everyone to share.
Developmental Stages:	To provide a healthy program in the life cycle of a group, the curriculum needs to offer courses on three levels of commitment: (1) Beginner Stage—low-level entry, high structure, to level the playing field; (2) Growth Stage—deeper Bible study, flexible structure, to encourage group accountability; (3) Discipleship Stage—in-depth Bible study, open structure, to move the group into high gear.
Target Audiences:	To build community throughout the culture of the church, the curriculum needs to be flexible, adaptable and transferable into the structure of the average church.

ACKNOWLEDGMENTS

To Zondervan Bible Publishers
for permission to use
the NIV text,
The Holy Bible, New International Bible Society.
© 1973, 1978, 1984 by International Bible Society.
Used by permission of Zondervan Bible Publishers.

WELCOME TO THE SERENDIPITY 301 DEPTH BIBLE STUDY SERIES

You are about to embark on an adventure into the powerful experience of depth Bible Study. The Serendipity 301 series combines three basic elements to produce a life-changing and group-changing course.

First, you will be challenged and enriched by the personal Bible Study that begins each unit. You will have the opportunity to dig into Scripture both for understanding and personal reflection. Although some groups may choose to do this section together at their meeting, doing it beforehand will greatly add to the experience of the course.

Second, you will benefit from the group sessions. Wonderful things happen when a small group of people get together and share their lives around the Word of God. Not only will you have a chance to take your personal study to a deeper level, you will have an opportunity to share on a deep level what's happening in your life and receive the encouragement and prayer support of your group.

Third, the 301 courses provide the stimulus and tools for your group to take steps toward fulfilling your group mission. Whether or not your group has gone through the preparation of a Serendipity 101 and 201 course, you can profit from this mission emphasis. The 32-page center section of this book will guide you through this process. And questions in the closing section of the group agenda will prompt your group to act upon the mission challenge to "give birth" to a new small group.

Put these three components together, and you have a journey in Christian discipleship well worth the effort. Enjoy God's Word! Enjoy genuine Christian community! Enjoy dreaming about your mission!

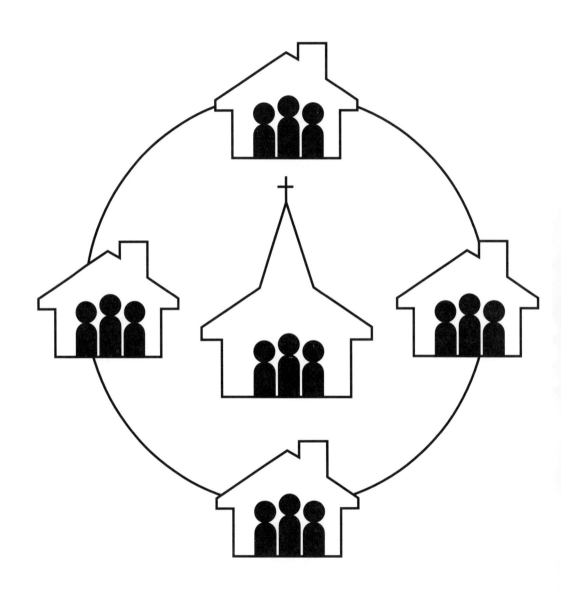

QUESTIONS & ANSWERS

STAGE

1. What stage in the life cycle of a small group is this course designed for?

Turn to the first page of the center section of this book. There you will see that this 301 course is designed for the third stage of a small group. In the Serendipity "Game Plan" for the multiplication of small groups, your group is in the Release Stage.

GOALS

2. What are the goals of a 301 study course?

As shown on the second page of the center section (page M2), the focus in this third stage is heavy on Bible Study and Mission.

BIBLE STUDY

301

3. What is the approach to Bible Study in this course?

This course involves two types of Bible Study. The "homework" assignment fosters growth in personal Bible study skills and in personal spiritual growth. The group study gives everyone a chance to share their learning and together take it to a deeper level.

SELF STUDY

4. What does the homework involve?

There are three parts to each assignment: (1) READ—to get the "bird's-eye view" of the passage and record your first impressions; (2) SEARCH—to get the "worm's-eye view" by digging into the passage verse-by-verse with specific questions; and (3) APPLY—to ask yourself, after studying the passage, "What am I going to do about it?"

THREE-STAGE LIFE CYCLE OF A GROUP

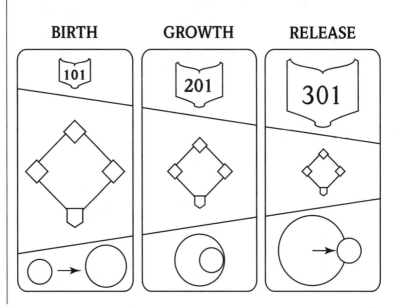

BIRTH   GROWTH   RELEASE

101   201   301

BIBLE KNOWLEDGE

5. *What if you don't know very much about the Bible?*

No problem. The homework assignment is designed to lead you step-by-step in your study. And there are study notes in each unit to give you help with key words, concepts and difficult passages.

AGENDA

6. *What is the agenda for the group meetings?*

The completed homework assignment becomes the basis for the group sharing. (However, those who don't do the homework should definitely be encouraged to come to the meeting anyway.) During the meeting the group will be guided to share on three levels: (1) TO BEGIN; (2) TO GO DEEPER; and (3) TO CLOSE.

STAYING ON TRACK

7. *How can the group get through all the material?*

Following the recommended time limits for each of the three sections will help keep you on track. Since you may not be able to answer all the questions with the time you have, you may need to skip some of them. Also, if you have more than seven people at a meeting, use the "Fearless Foursomes" described below for the Bible Study.

THE FEARLESS FOURSOME!

If you have more than seven people at a meeting, Serendipity recommends you divide into groups of 4 for the Bible Study. Count off around the group: "one, two, one, two, etc."—and have the "ones" move quickly to another room for the Bible Study. Ask one person to be the leader and follow the directions for the Bible Study time. After 30 minutes, the Group Leader will call "Time" and ask all groups to come together for the Caring Time.

GROUP BUILDING

8. *How does this course develop Group Building?*

Although this series is Serendipity's deepest Bible Study curriculum, Group Building is still essential. The group will continue "checking in" with each other and will challenge each other to grow in Christian discipleship. Working together on the group's mission should also be a very positive group-building process.

**MISSION /
MULTIPLICATION**

9. *What is the mission of a 301 group?*

   Page M3 of the center section summarizes the mission of groups using this course: to commission a team from your group to start a new group. The center section will lead your group in doing this.

**LEADERSHIP
TRAINING**

10. *How do we incorporate this mission into the course?*

    Page M5 of the center section gives an overview of the six steps in this process. You can either add this leadership training to the sessions a little bit at a time or in a couple of separate sessions.

**GROUP
COVENANT**

11. *What is a group covenant?*

    A group covenant is a "contract" that spells out your expectations and the ground rules for your group. It's very important that your group discuss these issues—preferably as part of the first session.

**GROUND
RULES**

12. *What are the ground rules for the group?* (Check those that you agree upon.)

    ❐ PRIORITY: While you are in the course, you give the group meetings priority.

    ❐ PARTICIPATION: Everyone participates and no one dominates.

    ❐ RESPECT: Everyone is given the right to their own opinion and all questions are encouraged and respected.

    ❐ CONFIDENTIALITY: Anything that is said in the meeting is never repeated outside the meeting.

    ❐ EMPTY CHAIR: The group stays open to new people at every meeting as long as they understand the ground rules.

    ❐ SUPPORT: Permission is given to call upon each other in time of need—even in the middle of the night.

    ❐ ADVICE GIVING: Unsolicited advice is not allowed.

    ❐ MISSION: We agree to do everything in our power to start a new group as our mission (see center section).

INTRODUCTION TO THE LIFE OF CHRIST

Jesus in History

There has never been anyone else like Jesus Christ. That, of course, is obvious to the Christian. But consider the view of the non-believer for a moment. They may not believe in Jesus' extraordinary powers and his claim to be the Son of God. But they are still left with a question that has mystified historians and philosophers for 2,000 years: Who was this man called Jesus Christ?

No one doubts that Jesus has had a profound influence on the world—more so than any other person. His story is a major theme of Western history. In fact, the events of history are measured by whether they happened before (B.C.) or after (A.D.) his birth. Explorers like Christopher Columbus, settlers like the Pilgrims, and missionaries like the Moravians and Franciscans were driven by a desire to honor God and claim new territory for Christ's kingdom. Many of the greatest works of Western art and music were created to honor Christ. King Richard the Lion-Hearted and others declared holy wars in his name, and activists such as Ghandi and Martin Luther King led peaceful protests based on Christ's example of nonviolence. Even adherents of Hinduism and Islam honor him as a great teacher.

In spite of Jesus' great influence, however, there is still a sense of mystery surrounding him. Who was Jesus? What was he like? These simple questions prompt a dizzying array of responses.

Different views of Jesus are clearly seen in films made over the years. The *Greatest Story Ever Told* (1965) pictures Jesus as an otherworldly figure, somewhat oddly intersecting with the world as we know it. He speaks King James English while everyone else talks like an American! In *Jesus Christ: Superstar* (1973), Jesus is portrayed as a discontented hippie, prone to strong emotions and outbursts of passion. Misunderstood by everyone else, he is not quite sure of himself either. The film *Jesus* (1979) presents a wise, gentle Jesus who patiently deals with the confusion everyone else experiences, while being clearly in control of his destiny.

While only one of these films (*Jesus*) was produced by a religious group, it is clear that even within circles of committed Christians there is wide diversity in terms of the way people understand Jesus. The way Jesus has been portrayed throughout history in art and literature reflects this. No North American congregation today would feel very comfortable if the front of their church were decorated with a portrait of Jesus flanked by the president of the United States and his wife. Yet frescoes of Jesus standing with contemporary kings and queens were common in churches throughout Europe during the middle centuries. This not only reflected a different view of church and state than North Americans have today. It also reflected a view of an ethereal Jesus whose rule over the cosmos was accompanied by all the trappings of earthly, materialistic power.

Church mosaics from even earlier periods picture Jesus as a Roman soldier, his cross wielded in his right arm like a sword. He is a conqueror, the leader of the church in its domination of the world with the Gospel. In sharp contrast, the Russian author Dostoevsky, in his novel *The Brothers Karamazov,* tells a tale of Jesus as a prisoner being tried and tortured by the church itself!

Many white Protestant Christians have traditionally identified Jesus with the fair-skinned, blue-eyed, hair-freshly-shampooed figure portrayed by Warner Sallman's famous "Head of Christ." This picture, found in prominent places in many churches, shows a calm, quiet, handsome man who (if he got a haircut and put on a suit) could easily fit in any Presbyterian or Lutheran church in America. However, many African-American Christians have a hard time believing that such a Jesus could relate at all to them. Likewise, white North American Christians are taken aback at portrayals of Jesus as black or Chinese.

Charles Sheldon's book *In His Steps*, a bestselling novel written at the end of the nineteenth century, imagines Jesus as a teacher of common sense and decency. To practice his way of life was certain to lead to the social respect, economic security, and good government that Americans so valued. This Jesus, however, has little in common with the Jesus of the poor communities in Latin America. There he is seen as one who sides with the poor in speaking out against those same social, economic and governmental forces of North America which survive, in part, by institutionalized oppression of underdeveloped countries. The contrast is similar to the way the Jesus of the white slaveholders (in the southern states in the early 1800s) was different from the one worshiped by their slaves.

Perhaps by now the point has been established: Coming to understand who Jesus is can be a difficult task! Everyone has some image of Jesus, through which they try to understand him. The questions, "Jesus Christ, Jesus Christ. Who are you? What have you sacrificed?"—which begin the theme song from the musical *Jesus Christ: Superstar*—continually need to be asked. Otherwise, we end up with a Jesus who is more a product of our culture than of Scripture.

Jesus in the Gospels

Jesus Christ: Superstar does not attempt to answer the critical questions which it raises, but the Gospels do. In fact, the Gospel of Mark—thought by most scholars to be the first Gospel—could be divided between these two questions: Mark 1–8 is built around the question, "Who is Jesus?" Chapters 9–16 look at the question, "Why did he come?"

The fact that the Gospel of Mark is framed to give insight to those two questions reveals something important about the Gospels. Although the Gospels are commonly thought of as biographies of Jesus, that is really not the case. A closer examination of the four Gospels reveals that the authors were not simply reporters, jotting down the day-to-day activities of Jesus. For instance, only Matthew and Luke have a birth narrative, and only Luke mentions anything at all about Jesus' childhood. John places the story of the raising of Lazarus as the climax of Jesus' identity and mission, yet none of the other Gospels even mention it. Some of the stories and teachings that the Gospels have in common are used to illustrate entirely different points. Close to a third of the material in each of the Gospels deals with the final week of Jesus' life.

This observation does not mean that the Gospels contradict one another or contain errors. What it does mean, however, is that the long-standing assumption that the Gospel authors were writing histories of Jesus is mistaken. It is far more useful to see the authors as theologians using narratives (or stories) as their means of teaching. As such, they were free to take the stories and sayings of Jesus (which were probably already well-known in the early church) and shape them in various ways to present Jesus in the way they felt their churches needed to see him. We simply do not have an untouched history of the life of Jesus; what we do have are four Spirit-inspired character sketches of his life, teachings and significance.

Perhaps a modern-day analogy will help clarify the intent of the authors of the Gospels. When the Democrats and Republicans meet at their national conventions to present their candidate for president, there will inevitably be a multi-media show about the candidate. In 1996, scenes from the life of Bill Clinton and Bob Dole were flashed before our eyes. Their childhood, their accomplishments, and the people with whom they associate were all reflected in some way. The scenes were all true. The producers undoubtedly used real pictures of real events in these men's lives. Yet there was no attempt to present these pictures in chronological order because the productions were not meant to be historical biographies. The pictures were organized around themes, not time. Their purpose was to communicate something of the character of candidate Dole and candidate Clinton so that you and I would vote for him. Had another producer arranged the show, he or she might have used the same images in a totally different progression in order to convey a different aspect of the candidate's personality. It would be foolish to say such presentations are false because scenes did not occur in chronological order. The producers never intended the show to be understood that way.

In the same way, the Gospel writers use scenes from the life of Jesus in order to present a picture of Jesus that will move their readers to respond in faith and obedience. Each Gospel is read as a separate work, each with its own perspective about who Jesus is and why he came.

The author of the fourth Gospel concluded by writing, "Jesus did many other things as well. If every one of them were written down, I suppose that even the whole world would not have room for the books that would be written" (John 21:25). Though exaggerated, the point is clear: that there was a wealth of information about Jesus that the author did *not* include! As a result, the stories we have about Jesus are not incidental. Each story is chosen and told in relation to the other stories in that Gospel to convey something either about the identity of Jesus or about the meaning of discipleship. Like the parables Jesus told or the miracles he performed, the incidents in the life of Jesus have a meaning beyond the story. The authors use these stories to provide theological insight regarding Jesus. In basic terms, the interests of each of the authors are as follows:

1. Matthew's interest is showing that Jesus is the long-awaited Messiah. Notable in his narrative is the repeated phrase "this was to fulfill what was written ..." by which he relates events in Jesus' life to Jewish prophecy (1:22; 2:5,17,23; 3:3; 4:14–16; 5:17–18; 8:17; 11:4–6; 12:17–21; 13:35; 21:4–5; 26:31). In addition, Matthew has five major blocks of teaching which form a manual about the kingdom of God (5:1–7:27: The Character of the Disciple; 10:1–42: The Preaching of the Kingdom; 13:1–52: Parables of the Kingdom; 18:1–35: Relationships in the Kingdom; 23:1–25:46: The Judgment of the Kingdom). Matthew wants to help his fellow Jews understand Jesus as God's Messiah of the new kingdom, whom they should follow in discipleship.

2. Mark, the shortest Gospel, highlights the actions of Jesus as a means of demonstrating his identity. Mark's terse, fast-moving style compels the reader to see Jesus as a person of enormous authority. The realization of that keeps people amazed and asking the question, "Who is he?" (1:27; 2:7,12; 4:41; 5:20,42; 6:51; 7:37; 8:29). Mark wants his readers to see Jesus as the incarnate Lord, the "Son of God," who came to redeem people from sin.

3. Luke's concern is to stress that the coming of Jesus means good news for all peoples, especially those who are considered insignificant by their culture. Shepherds, children, women, and "sinners" of all types figure prominently. Luke alone tells the story of the sinful woman who anointed Jesus' feet with her tears (7:36–50) and includes the Parable of the Prodigal Son (15:11–32), both of which typify his interest in God's love for the "outsider."

4. John's Gospel is very different from the other three. The chronology is vastly different (as is his style). Jesus engages in long dialogues and monologues not found in the other Gospels. Seven miracles, most of which are not found in the other Gospels, form the framework upon which the author builds his Gospel. The death of Jesus is never far from view, even in the first chapter, in which Jesus is identified as "the Lamb of God, who takes away the sin of the world" (1:29). John wants his readers to see Jesus as God in the flesh (1:14; 8:58; 20:28); he has come to give his life so that all who entrust themselves to him might have life.

The fact that each Gospel has a different emphasis is an advantage for us. Our understanding of Jesus is broader than it could ever be if we had only one source. But sometimes we can become so preoccupied with the differences in the Gospels that we lose sight of the meaning. For instance, many writers have worked out a way to explain the seeming differences in the order of events in the life of Christ. But it is very important that we do not stop there. We need to interpret the stories in a given Gospel in light of the overall emphasis of that particular Gospel. Let each author tell his own story.

The Purpose of These Studies
Given this background, the studies in this booklet should not be approached as a "harmony" of the Gospels. While the material has been arranged in a logical order (beginning with Luke's birth story and ending with Matthew's account of the Resurrection), the point is not to try to present a

history of Jesus. Instead, these studies are more like snapshots in a photograph album. Each snapshot tells an important story about Jesus. The notes accompanying each study provide some of the context to aid the reader's understanding of the story in relationship to the overall thrust of the particular Gospel in which it is found.

Reading the Gospels is not like reading other biographies. The study of these 13 selections from the Gospels will give the reader a sense of some of the important events in the life of Jesus. But the main purpose of these passages is to lead readers into a greater understanding of the meaning of Jesus' life and its implications for their own. What may start as an interest in a famous person of history becomes an exercise in self-evaluation and decision making.

We will personally have to wrestle with the question "Who is Jesus?" We will especially have to confront the ways in which our views of Jesus are more colored by our particular culture than by the meaning of the stories we have about him.

We will also have to wrestle with our response to Jesus. Too often, people look to the Gospels (and the Bible as a whole) only as a source of comfort and assurance. In reality, a great deal of the Bible is meant to provoke precisely the opposite reactions! The Gospels do not give us the option of holding a polite, distant admiration of Jesus as a wonderful religious teacher. Instead, they call for us to think and live differently. We have to change and be ready to keep on changing as the implications of discipleship unfold before us and become clear. A continual, thoughtful reading of the Gospels will not reinforce any long-held image of Jesus. The picture is more like looking at an object through a kaleidoscope. We will find a dynamic, multi-faceted character whose identity and teaching cannot be captured by any one description.

The story is told of a British commentator who wrote an insightful article about the meaning of James 2:1–4. In this passage, James warns the church not to show favor toward the rich. For instance, James specifically attacks the custom of reserving the best seats for the wealthy, while the poor are made to stand in the back or sit on the floor. The commentator, upon completing a detailed exposition of this passage, concluded with the assurance that this teaching did not apply to the then-common practice in English churches of having the affluent members of the church sit in the best seats, while poorer members were kept in the back! The commentator's cultural blinders led him to deny what certainly appears to be precisely the point of the text for the life of the church!

It's easy to fault the commentator, but will we do better? Will we listen to the message of the Gospels, even when that message threatens *our* traditional assumptions and practices? That question presses in on us in a variety of ways throughout these stories, throughout the Gospels, and throughout all of Scripture. Reading and reflecting upon the life of Jesus is a dangerous habit! It will continually force us to deal with the basic challenge of the Christian faith: In light of what you understand about Jesus, how will you follow him now?

UNIT 1—The Birth of Jesus / Luke 2:1-20

The Birth of Jesus

2 *In those days Caesar Augustus issued a decree that a census should be taken of the entire Roman world. ²(This was the first census that took place while Quirinius was governor of Syria.) ³And everyone went to his own town to register.*

⁴So Joseph also went up from the town of Nazareth in Galilee to Judea, to Bethlehem the town of David, because he belonged to the house and line of David. ⁵He went there to register with Mary, who was pledged to be married to him and was expecting a child. ⁶While they were there, the time came for the baby to be born, ⁷and she gave birth to her firstborn, a son. She wrapped him in cloths and placed him in a manger, because there was no room for them in the inn.

The Shepherds and the Angels

⁸And there were shepherds living out in the fields nearby, keeping watch over their flocks at night. ⁹An angel of the Lord appeared to them, and the glory of the Lord shone around them, and they were terrified. ¹⁰But the angel said to them, "Do not be afraid. I bring you good news of great joy that will be for all the people. ¹¹Today in the town of David a Savior has been born to you; he is Christ the Lord. ¹²This will be a sign to you: You will find a baby wrapped in cloths and lying in a manger."

¹³Suddenly a great company of the heavenly host appeared with the angel, praising God and saying,

¹⁴"Glory to God in the highest,
and on earth peace to men on whom
his favor rests."

¹⁵When the angels had left them and gone into heaven, the shepherds said to one another, "Let's go to Bethlehem and see this thing that has happened, which the Lord has told us about."

¹⁶So they hurried off and found Mary and Joseph, and the baby, who was lying in the manger. ¹⁷When they had seen him, they spread the word concerning what had been told them about this child, ¹⁸and all who heard it were amazed at what the shepherds said to them. ¹⁹But Mary treasured up all these things and pondered them in her heart. ²⁰The shepherds returned, glorifying and praising God for all the things they had heard and seen, which were just as they had been told.

READ

Two readings of the passage are suggested—each with a response to be checked or filled in on the worksheet.

First Reading / First Impressions: If you were the editor of *Time Magazine* and had to put this story in an appropriate section, which would you choose?

☒ World News   ☐ Science   ☐ Book Reviews
☐ Religion   ☐ People   ☐ other:_____

Second Reading / Big Idea: If you were a newspaper reporter writing a story about the events of this night, how might you write your headline?

Salvation Was Born Tonight

SEARCH

1. Why do you suppose the Savior of the world was born in an obscure village like Bethlehem—and even laid in a manger?

To fulfill prophecy from OT

2. Of all the people God could have chosen to announce his Son's birth to, why do you think he chose shepherds (see note on v. 8)?

Typically God used the least in a profound way.

3. Verse 11 contains three titles for Jesus. What does each one mean (see notes)?

Savior: *the One who saves His people from sin & death.*

Christ: *Messiah, the annointed One*

Lord: *Title implies His absolute authority & His diety*

4. According to verse 14, what would the birth of this baby bring to God? To earth?

Bring honor to God. Personal & relational harmony to the people He has called.

5. In verses 15–20, the events of the evening come to a close. What reactions do you see in the following people?

the shepherds: *rejoiced, glorifying & praising God for what they saw & heard fulfilling OT prophecy*

the townspeople: *They were amazed.*

Mary: *saw herself greatly blessed & a lowly servant*

APPLY

1. As you begin this course, what are some goals you would like to work on? Check one or two from the list below and add another if you wish.
   - ☑ to get to know God in a more personal way
   - ☐ to understand what I believe as a Christian and where I stand on issues
   - ☑ to develop my skills in Bible study and personal devotions
   - ☐ to belong to a small group that will support me in my growth
   - ☑ to think through my values and priorities in light of God's will
   - ☐ to wrestle with the next step in my spiritual journey

2. What are you willing to commit to in the way of disciplines during the time you are in this course?
   - ☑ to complete the Bible study home assignment before the group meets
   - ☑ to attend the group meetings except in cases of emergency
   - ☑ to share in leading the group—taking my turn in rotation
   - ☑ to keep confidential anything that is shared in the group
   - ☑ to reach out to others who are not in a group and invite them to join us
   - ☑ to participate in the group's mission of "giving birth" to a new group (see center section)

GROUP AGENDA

Every group meeting has three parts: (1) To Begin (10–15 minutes) to break the ice; (2) To Go Deeper (30 minutes) for Bible Study; and (3) To Close (15–30 minutes) for caring and prayer. When you get to the second part, have someone read the Scripture out loud and then divide into groups of 4 (4 at the dining table, 4 at the kitchen table, etc.). Then have everyone come back together for the third part.

TO BEGIN / 10–15 Min. (Choose 1 or 2)
1. What do you know about your own birth?
2. If you are a parent, what are some stories you could tell about the birth of your first child?
3. What is your favorite thing about Christmas?

TO GO DEEPER / 30 Min. (Choose 2 or 3)
1. Let each person choose one of the READ or SEARCH questions from the "homework" to answer. (It's okay if more than one person chooses the same question.)
2. The author Luke was a physician. Why do you think he would be so careful in his account of Jesus' birth?
3. In what ways might verse 14 be a good summary of what Jesus' mission was all about?
4. This course, as the four Gospels, is like a photograph album—each snapshot telling a significant story about Jesus. What are a couple of the most important snapshots in the photo album of *your* spiritual life? Specifically, what was your spiritual birth or beginning like?
5. What effect does the news of Christ's birth have on you *now*? How do you feel about your current relationship with God's Son?

TO CLOSE / 15–30 Min.
1. What did you check under APPLY for the goals you would like to work on during this course?
2. What disciplines are you willing to commit to (second question in APPLY)?
3. How can the group pray for you?

NOTES

Summary. The story of Jesus begins with his birth. As Luke's account indicates, this was no ordinary birth. God was about to visit the planet. It is amazing that of all the ways God could have come—as the invincible King riding on a chariot of fire, as a Voice of Declaration out of the heavens, as a great Being of Light—he chooses to come as a helpless baby born of a woman. Thus the story begins with God's incarnation: the eternal, pre-existent Word of God becomes flesh and lives for a while among us (John 1:14). This is the third of three visions of angels that are found in Luke's story of the birth of Christ (to Zechariah: 1:5–24; to Mary: 1:26–38; and to the shepherds: 2:8–20). The irony and grace of the Gospel is captured here as the angel declares the majesty and glory of Jesus and his mission to poor men and women of no status. The Lord of the universe is born in a stable to a peasant girl.

2:1 *Caesar Augustus.* Luke roots Christ's birth firmly in history. Augustus, originally known as Gaius Octavius (or Octavian) ruled the Roman Empire from 30 B.C. to A.D. 14. Augustus was a wise ruler who encouraged the arts and built many fine projects. He also brought an unprecedented period of peace to the world.

census. From about 30 B.C. onward, the Caesars ordered people in the various Roman provinces to report every 14 years for a census for tax purposes. Resistance from the population and from local rulers sometimes meant census-taking that took several years to complete.

2:3 *everyone went to his own town.* Generally people were taxed where they lived. If you had property elsewhere, however, you had to go there to register. So it seems that Joseph had some property in Bethlehem.

2:4 *Bethlehem.* Bethlehem was some 90 miles from Nazareth, a three or four day journey. Joseph was from the line of David and Bethlehem was the city of David, so this is where Joseph's family and clan would have lived (which is why he would have had property there).

2:5 *to register with Mary.* Normally only the head of the household needed to register. However, in some Roman provinces all women over 12 were required to pay a poll tax, and this may have been the reason Mary accompanied Joseph on this trip.

pledged to be married to him and was expecting a child. Their betrothal had not yet been consummated by intercourse (see Matt. 1:24–25). Luke 1:26–38 records the announcement by the angel to Mary that she would conceive a child through the agency of the Holy Spirit.

2:6–7 While in Bethlehem, the time for birth arrived. Thus the political decision of the Roman emperor led to the fulfillment of the prophecy in Micah 5:2: "But you, Bethlehem Ephrathah, though you are small among the clans of Judah, out of you will come for me one who will be ruler over Israel."

2:7 *manger.* This was a feeding trough for animals.

the inn. This word can mean either a building used for the accommodation of travelers or a spare room in a private home. Whichever the case, there was no space available for the couple in normal lodgings. Instead, they stayed with the animals. A tradition dating back to the second century maintains this was in a cave over which today is the Church of the Nativity.

2:8 *shepherds.* Shepherds were economically, socially and religiously "low-class" people. Since the temple authorities kept flocks of sheep for sacrifices pastured near Bethlehem, it might be that the shepherds of these particular flocks were the ones visited by the angels. So it was to shepherds that the great announcement was made—not to kings nor to priests nor to the wealthy nor even to the religious— but it was to lower-class working men that the angel of the Lord appeared to announce the birth of the Savior.

2:9 *An angel of the Lord.* "The angel of the Lord ... is represented as a heavenly being sent by God to deal with people as his personal agent and spokesman" (*The New Bible Dictionary*). In some OT passages, the angel of the Lord is virtually identified as God himself (Gen. 16:7ff; Ex. 3:2; Judges 6:11ff), indicating his divine authority and splendor. Popular thought often pictures angels as chubby, cute, naked children, but the Bible consistently represents them as supernatural creatures of enormous power and majesty. Throughout the Bible, angels serve as God's agents of instruction, judgment and deliverance.

the glory of the Lord. This is the overwhelmingly powerful light that accompanies the presence of God (Ps. 104:1–2; Ezek. 1).

they were terrified. In the Bible, whenever an angel appears, people are terrified. It is the fear of being in the presence of something supernatural, powerful and totally foreign to one's experience (Luke 1:29–30; Ex. 3:2–6; Dan. 10:7).

2:10 *Do not be afraid.* The angel has not come to frighten them, but to announce God's good news to them.

I bring you good news of great joy. The form of the angel's message is similar to that used to announce the birth of Roman kings.

all the people. The Savior has come not just for Jews but for all people. This is an important theme in the Gospel of Luke. God's mercy includes the Gentiles; the Gospel is universal, not particular.

2:11 *a Savior ... Christ the Lord.* The angel gives a full-orbed description of the roles which this child will play.

Savior. In the Old Testament, this term only applied to God (Isa. 43:3,11). God's deliverance of Israel (first from Egypt and then, centuries later, from Babylon), illustrates that the title is meant to honor God as the one who rescues his people from an otherwise unbeatable foe. This title was ascribed to Jesus as the one who saves his people from sin and death.

Christ. This is the Greek word for the Hebrew title, Messiah. Both terms mean "the Anointed One." In Jewish thought, this meant the prophesied king of Israel who would deliver Israel from bondage into an era of freedom, power, influence and prosperity.

Lord. This is a very common title used for God in the OT. It implies both his absolute authority and his deity. In the NT this is the most often used title for Jesus as well, emphasizing his deity and authority.

2:14 *Glory to God in the highest.* The angelic chorus sings of how Jesus' birth will bring honor to God and personal and relational harmony to people whom he has called.

peace to men on whom his favor rests. While older versions divide this phrase into two clauses (peace on earth / good will toward men), the NIV translation is to be preferred. There are not two statements of God's wishes for humanity, but a clear promise of peace to those who receive God's grace.

2:17 *they spread the word.* Luke is concerned throughout his Gospel (as well as in Acts) to show that the message of Christ is to be taken to all people. The shepherds become the first witnesses.

2:19 *Mary treasured up all these things and pondered them in her heart.* The words used to describe Mary's response indicate deep thought and reflection in an attempt to understand.

15

UNIT 2—Baptism and Temptation / Matt. 3:13-4:11

The Baptism of Jesus

¹³Then Jesus came from Galilee to the Jordan to be baptized by John. ¹⁴But John tried to deter him, saying, "I need to be baptized by you, and do you come to me?"

¹⁵Jesus replied, "Let it be so now; it is proper for us to do this to fulfill all righteousness." Then John consented.

¹⁶As soon as Jesus was baptized, he went up out of the water. At that moment heaven was opened, and he saw the Spirit of God descending like a dove and lighting on him. ¹⁷And a voice from heaven said, "This is my Son, whom I love; with him I am well pleased."

The Temptation of Jesus

4 Then Jesus was led by the Spirit into the desert to be tempted by the devil. ²After fasting forty days and forty nights, he was hungry. ³The tempter came to him and said, "If you are the Son of God, tell these stones to become bread."

⁴Jesus answered, "It is written: 'Man does not live on bread alone, but on every word that comes from the mouth of God.' "

⁵Then the devil took him to the holy city and had him stand on the highest point of the temple. ⁶"If you are the Son of God," he said, "throw yourself down. For it is written:

" 'He will command his angels concerning you,
    and they will lift you up in their hands,
so that you will not strike your foot against a
    stone.' "

⁷Jesus answered him, "It is also written: 'Do not put the Lord your God to the test.' "

⁸Again, the devil took him to a very high mountain and showed him all the kingdoms of the world and their splendor. ⁹"All this I will give you," he said, "if you will bow down and worship me."

¹⁰Jesus said to him, "Away from me, Satan! For it is written: 'Worship the Lord your God, and serve him only.' "

¹¹Then the devil left him, and angels came and attended him.

READ

First Reading / First Impressions: What relationship do you initially see between these stories?

❏ A contrast between a high and low point in Jesus' life.

❏ A continuation that simply affirms Jesus' identity and purpose in different ways.

❏ A cause-and-effect situation in which God's affirmation of Jesus resulted in an especially strong satanic attack.

❏ A progression which climaxes in Jesus' clear statement of loyalty to God.

❏ other:_____

Second Reading / Big Idea: How vulnerable to temptation was Jesus?

❏ He was just as vulnerable as I am.

❏ He was vulnerable, but in a different way.

❏ He really wasn't vulnerable at all.

SEARCH

1. John was baptizing people as a sign of their repentance from sin. Since Jesus had no sin, what might be the significance of his baptism (3:13–15; see notes)?

2. What do you think 3:17 meant to Jesus? How does this set the stage for his ministry to begin?

3. Consider the temptations in 4:1–10 (and the notes for these verses). For each of them: (a) What is the human need or desire that is the basis for the appeal? (b) What makes the action wrong in this instance? (c) How does Jesus respond?

	Temptation #1	Temptation #2	Temptation #3
need / desire			
why wrong			
Jesus' response			

4. When you look at these two events (which occur at the beginning of Jesus' ministry), what do you learn about the character of Jesus?

APPLY

1. If the devil had three "shots" at you, which area of your life would he focus on?
   - ❏ spiritual temptations
   - ❏ physical temptations
   - ❏ ambition / power
   - ❏ my self-identity
   - ❏ my relationships
   - ❏ other:_____

2. In light of Jesus' example in this story, what would help you resist these temptations?

3. Read Hebrews 4:14–16 and then make it into a brief prayer of commitment or thanksgiving.

GROUP AGENDA

Every group meeting has three parts: (1) To Begin (10–15 minutes) to break the ice; (2) To Go Deeper (30 minutes) for Bible Study; and (3) To Close (15–30 minutes) for caring and prayer. When you get to the second part, have someone read the Scripture out loud and then divide into groups of 4 (4 at the dining table, 4 at the kitchen table, etc.). Then have everyone come back together for the third part.

TO BEGIN / 10–15 Min. (Choose 1 or 2)

1. What is the closest you have come to a "rite of passage" in your life?

2. Who was there for you at a critical time in your life—giving you encouragement?

3. What are you tempted by that is either fattening or expensive?

TO GO DEEPER / 30 Min. (Choose 2 or 3)

1. If you have completed the READ and SEARCH sections, what stands out the most to you from the questions or study notes?

2. In what way was Jesus' baptism and temptation his "rite of passage"? Why do you think he had to go through this?

3. Jesus was about 30 at this time and just starting his "career." Why would these particular temptations be attractive to him?

4. When have you been in the "wilderness"—severely tempted or tested?

5. CASE STUDY: Your friend confides in you about his/her intense struggle with a secret addiction. What can you say to help?

TO CLOSE / 15–30 Min.

1. Who could you invite to this group next week?

2. If you feel comfortable doing so, share your responses to the first two questions in APPLY.

3. How can the group pray for you, especially in the area of temptation?

4. In closing the prayer time, let those who would like to share the prayer they wrote in APPLY.

NOTES

Summary. Little is known of Jesus' childhood except for the story of his visit to the temple with his parents when Jesus was 12 years old (Luke 2:41–52). Beyond this we know nothing. However, certain nonbiblical texts sought to "fill in the gaps," as it were. They tell wondrous tales of Jesus as a little boy who made clay birds come alive and fly and turned his playmates into goats. These stories are clearly products of overworked imaginations and add nothing to our true knowledge of Jesus. In the Gospels, in fact, the story of Jesus jumps from his birth right to his ministry. Matthew, Luke and Mark all begin the public ministry of Jesus with his baptism and temptation. At his baptism, he is affirmed as God's beloved Son. Through the temptation he is portrayed as the true servant of God.

3:13 *baptized.* Whether this was done by immersion, by pouring, or by sprinkling is uncertain. All were considered forms of ceremonial washings that could be generally called baptisms. By allowing himself to be baptized, Jesus both identifies with the sin of his people (prefiguring his death for sin a few years hence) and proclaims his radical allegiance to God (an allegiance that will be tested through his temptations).

3:15 *to fulfill all righteousness.* "In the context of Jesus' baptism, the word 'righteousness' refers to the righteousness of life which was demanded of those who accepted that baptism; by submitting to John's baptism, Jesus acknowledged this standard of righteousness as valid both for himself and for others, and affirms that he will realize it and establish it ("fulfill") as the will of God in the Kingdom" (Hill).

3:16 *like a dove.* Matthew uses the symbol of a dove to communicate the coming of the Holy Spirit. Just what happened can never be fully known. The dove was not a common symbol in first-century Israel. However, even if the nature of the event is uncertain, its meaning is clear: this is the promised anointing of the Messiah with the Holy Spirit (see Isa. 11:2; 42:1; 61:1).

3:17 *a voice.* Whether or not the voice is heard by the crowds is not clear. The form of the statement—"This is my Son"—seems to indicate that others may have heard it. These words are an unqualified affirmation of Jesus as he is about to launch his ministry. In the days ahead, it will be Jesus' task to make known to Israel who he is.

4:1 *led by the Spirit.* The same Spirit who had come to Jesus in such affirming power, now sends him forth to this time of testing.

tempted. This word always means "test" in Matthew. This was a trial of strength in which Satan's intent was to get Jesus to renounce his identity as the anointed one of God.

the devil. Satan does not figure prominently *per se* in the Old Testament (although the New Testament identifies the serpent in the Garden of Eden as Satan—Rev. 12:9; see also Job 1:6; Zech. 3:2). But in later Jewish thought (and in the NT) he is portrayed as an angel who has rebelled against God and is set against God's purposes and people.

4:2 forty days. Moses fasted for 40 days on Mount Sinai while receiving the commandments (Ex. 34:28), and Israel was in the wilderness 40 years (Deut. 8:2). Matthew pictures Jesus as the new Moses and the new Israel.

4:3 The tempter came. The Spirit led Jesus into the wilderness, but it is Satan who tests him. His challenges to Jesus come only after Jesus has entered a condition of physical weakness.

If you are the Son of God. "If" should be understood in the sense of "since." Satan begins by challenging the need for the Son of God to fast at all. Why not simply use his divine power to end his hunger? This was a temptation to verify the truth of what God had declared (3:17).

bread. Satan's suggestion is not evil in itself, but in the context of this test, it would be like Israel's complaining that God had not adequately met their needs in the desert (Ex. 16). Rather than trust God, the temptation is for Jesus to take matters into his own hands.

4:4 Jesus' response is drawn from Deuteronomy 8:3, which was originally a reflection on the meaning of the manna in the desert. True life is found not through food ("bread alone"), but through the words of God. Jesus will not heed Satan, but listen only to his Father. God, who brought manna to Israel, also led them to hunger so that they might learn dependence upon him alone. This was the reason for Jesus' time in the desert as well. Israel complained, but Jesus will trust God to provide when it is appropriate.

4:5 the highest point of the temple. Barclay says this would have been a point about 450 feet above the Kedron Valley. The temple was the focal point in Israel of God's love and power. The challenge is to prove this love and power by creating a peril from which only God can rescue him. This would be a display that would gain the attention of the people, who would then recognize that Jesus has the rightful claim to the title "Messiah."

4:6 If you are the Son of God. Once again the challenge is to demonstrate that Jesus is the Messiah.

For it is written. Satan now quotes Psalm 91:11–12 to prove his case. The difference in the way Jesus and Satan use Scripture is instructive. Jesus uses quotes that sum up central truths found throughout the Old Testament Scripture. Satan wrests this quote from its context to manipulate it to mean something very different. Psalm 91:11–12 is a promise that God will be with his people in the midst of difficult times. Satan misapplies this promise to try to get Jesus to do something that would be foolhardy in an attempt to force God to act.

4:7 Jesus recognizes the manipulative tactic of Satan and responds to him with a quote from Deuteronomy 6:16. That verse refers to an incident from Exodus 17:1–7, in which the people essentially gave Moses an ultimatum to prove whether "the Lord is among us or not." Jesus refuses to question the presence and protection of God as Israel did.

4:8–9 The final temptation has to do with gaining the kingdoms of the world without suffering the coming agonies of the cross.

4:9 All this I will give you. Satan offers Jesus a painless, immediate way to power and fame. In fact, by his obedience to the Father, Jesus *would* become the King of kings possessing all authority and power (Ps. 2:8; Dan. 7:14).

if you will bow down and worship me. This would involve a definite turning from God to Satan. While Israel turned to idols in the desert (Ex. 32), Jesus refuses to turn from God.

4:10 Jesus quotes Deuteronomy 6:13 to affirm his allegiance to God and to reject Satan's offer. Such loyalty precluded any consideration of Satan's means to gain that power. Satan had appealed to Jesus' legitimate needs (v. 3), his insecurities (vv. 6–7), and his ambitions (v. 8), but had failed to overcome Jesus' loyalty to God. In the face of that resolve, Satan was powerless to dissuade Jesus.

4:11 angels came and attended him. One function of angels is to bring comfort and aid to God's people (Heb. 1:14). Thus prepared by his baptism and his temptation, Jesus begins his ministry (Matt. 4:12–17).

UNIT 3—Jesus Begins His Ministry / Luke 4:14-30

Jesus Rejected at Nazareth

¹⁴Jesus returned to Galilee in the power of the Spirit, and news about him spread through the whole countryside. ¹⁵He taught in their synagogues, and everyone praised him.

¹⁶He went to Nazareth, where he had been brought up, and on the Sabbath day he went into the synagogue, as was his custom. And he stood up to read. ¹⁷The scroll of the prophet Isaiah was handed to him. Unrolling it, he found the place where it is written:

¹⁸"The Spirit of the Lord is on me,
    because he has anointed me
    to preach good news to the poor.
He has sent me to proclaim freedom for the prisoners
    and recovery of sight for the blind,
to release the oppressed,
¹⁹   to proclaim the year of the Lord's favor."

²⁰Then he rolled up the scroll, gave it back to the attendant and sat down. The eyes of everyone in the synagogue were fastened on him, ²¹and he began by saying to them, "Today this scripture is fulfilled in your hearing."

²²All spoke well of him and were amazed at the gracious words that came from his lips. "Isn't this Joseph's son?" they asked.

²³Jesus said to them, "Surely you will quote this proverb to me: 'Physician, heal yourself! Do here in your hometown what we have heard that you did in Capernaum.' "

²⁴"I tell you the truth," he continued, "no prophet is accepted in his hometown. ²⁵I assure you that there were many widows in Israel in Elijah's time, when the sky was shut for three and a half years and there was a severe famine throughout the land. ²⁶Yet Elijah was not sent to any of them, but to a widow in Zarephath in the region of Sidon. ²⁷And there were many in Israel with leprosy in the time of Elisha the prophet, yet not one of them was cleansed—only Naaman the Syrian."

²⁸All the people in the synagogue were furious when they heard this. ²⁹They got up, drove him out of the town, and took him to the brow of the hill on which the town was built, in order to throw him down the cliff. ³⁰But he walked right through the crowd and went on his way.

READ

First Reading / First Impressions: What headline would you expect to see in the Nazareth newspaper after these events?

- ❏ "Local Man Returns With Big Claims"
- ❏ "False Prophet Spews Anti-Semitic Rhetoric"
- ☒ "Synagogue Scene Turns Violent"
- ❏ "Antagonizing Preacher Narrowly Escapes Mob"

Second Reading / Big Idea: What is one major impression you have of Jesus' personality from this incident?

- ❏ self-assured
- ❏ abrasive
- ❏ confrontational
- ❏ perplexing
- ❏ passionate
- ☒ focused
- ❏ uncompromising
- ❏ other:_____

SEARCH

1. In the Scripture in the last unit, Jesus was led by the Holy Spirit to be tempted in the desert. What was the role of the Spirit now that Jesus was beginning his public ministry (v. 14; see notes)?

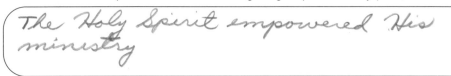

The Holy Spirit empowered His ministry

2. Imagine that you are a Jew and have just heard Jesus read a familiar passage that is central to your national dreams and hopes (vv. 18–19). What type of speech would you expect to hear as a result?

☐ a rousing one, stirring my hopes

☒ a comforting one, assuring me of God's future plans

☐ a stirring one, calling me to take action against the Roman oppressors

☐ a soothing one, based on nostalgic memories of past greatness

☐ other:_____

3. How did Jesus fulfill this five-fold mission, spoken of by Isaiah, during his ministry (see note on v. 21)?

Because He was there to bring it about.

4. How does he continue to fulfill it now?

5. Jesus uses two proverbs and two Old Testament stories to make his point in verses 23–27. In plain language, rephrase what Jesus is saying to the people in this section. Why do you think Jesus would deliberately hit this "hot button"?

APPLY

1. Which of the following five ministries of Jesus do you have a need for in your own life—either literally and physically or symbolically and spiritually?

☐ good news to the poor ☐ recovery of sight for the blind

☐ freedom for the prisoners ☐ release for the oppressed

☐ proclaiming the year of the Lord's favor (celebrating God's grace to "debtors")

2. In which of the five ministries do you feel God is calling you to invest yourself in serving others?

3. Jesus' hometown people couldn't see how God could care for Gentiles. What prejudices limit you and your church's ability to minister in God's name to those outside of your own circle?

21

GROUP AGENDA

Every group meeting has three parts: (1) To Begin (10–15 minutes) to break the ice; (2) To Go Deeper (30 minutes) for Bible Study; and (3) To Close (15–30 minutes) for caring and prayer. When you get to the second part, have someone read the Scripture out loud and then divide into groups of 4 (4 at the dining table, 4 at the kitchen table, etc.). Then have everyone come back together for the third part.

TO BEGIN / 10–15 Min. (Choose 1 or 2)
1. What did you like best about the community where you grew up? What did you like least?

2. Would you like to go back to that community to live? How would you be received?

3. When have you received a "Dear John" letter (or similar rejection)?

TO GO DEEPER / 30 Min. (Choose 2 or 3)
1. Based on the homework questions and the study notes, what do you learn from this passage about Jesus' self-understood mission?

2. Why did the people in Jesus' hometown reject him?

3. How do you imagine Jesus felt when he arrived in Nazareth? When he was rejected there?

4. How do you deal with feelings of rejection: Withdraw and mope? Strike back? Get hardened by them? Try to laugh them off? Talk about them? Pray about them?

5. How comfortable do you feel sharing your struggles with this group? How do feelings of rejection affect your participation in a group like this?

6. CASE STUDY: Jim grew up in a strict religious home. He went to a Christian school, but rebelled in college and married a non-Christian. His wife became a Christian in your Bible study group and now wants Jim to join the group. What should the group do?

TO CLOSE / 15–30 Min.
1. As a way of continuing the ministry of Jesus (vv. 18–19), has your group started on the six steps toward fulfilling your mission—from the center section?

2. How did you answer the questions in APPLY?

3. How can the group help you this week in prayer?

NOTES

Summary. Having affirmed his loyalty and faithfulness to God in a way that Israel had not been able to do, Jesus emerges from the wilderness empowered by God's Spirit to begin his ministry. As this passage shows, the response to Jesus' ministry was mixed. On the one hand, his ministry was highly popular with the crowds, as might be expected in a day in which there was little reliable medical care (and Jesus effectively healed a variety of diseases); in which little could be done about demon possession (and Jesus effectively cast out all manner of demons); and in which the rabbinic teaching was pedantic and boring (while Jesus was praised as a powerful teacher). On the other hand, he was opposed by the people in his own hometown (who scorned him as one who pretended—in their view—to be someone he could not possibly be) and the religious leaders (who feared Jesus because he did not follow their ways—see Unit 5).

4:14 *Galilee*. From 4:14–9:50, Luke records Jesus' ministry in Galilee, a province about 50 miles long and 25 miles wide in the north of Palestine.

in the power of the Spirit. Just as the Spirit led Jesus into his time of testing (Matt. 4:1; Luke 4:1), so the Spirit now empowers Jesus' ministry. Luke especially emphasizes the role of Jesus as the bearer of God's Spirit in fullness.

news about him spread. Jesus' initial ministry of healing, exorcism and teaching (Mark 1:21–39) met with enormous popular support in Galilee.

4:15 *synagogues*. While the temple in Jerusalem was the religious center for all Jews, the community synagogue was the focal point of weekly worship and teaching. Jesus' initial ministry was as a well-received itinerant preacher teaching in synagogues throughout Galilee. It is in the light of stories of his healings and teachings that he comes to his hometown of Nazareth.

4:16 *Nazareth*. Nazareth, a town of about 20,000 people, was located in a hollow surrounded by hills.

the Sabbath. Each Sabbath, Jews would gather at the synagogue for a service of worship and instruction from the Scripture. There was a standard order governing which passages of the Law would be read, and the same may have been true about the reading from the Prophets as well. The synagogue had no formal clergy, so various men approved by the elders of the synagogue read and taught from the Scripture. Given Jesus' emerging reputation, it is not surprising that he was asked to read and teach.

4:18 The passage Jesus read was from Isaiah 61:1–2 (with the addition of a phrase from 58:6). Using the metaphors of people in prison, blindness and slavery, the prophet speaks of his God-given mission to proclaim freedom and pardon to people who are oppressed and burdened.

The Spirit of the Lord is on me. The ministry of a prophet of God is one empowered by God's Spirit.

to preach good news / to proclaim freedom / recovery of sight. In the context of the Isaiah passage, this was the news that God was going to deliver the Jews from their captivity in Babylon. In later Judaism, it became the hope for Israel's ultimate restoration and freedom from all oppressors. The "recovery of sight" in Isaiah's sense probably meant the renewal of hope that was lost through the destruction and deportation of the Jews, or the sense that prisoners who had long been locked up would now be free to see the light of day.

release the oppressed. These words are not found in either the Hebrew or Greek versions of Isaiah 61, but may be borrowed from a phrase in Isaiah 58:6 as a commentary on the meaning of the "recovery of sight."

4:19 the year of the Lord's favor. This specifically refers to the Jubilee Year of Leviticus 25. Every 50 years, the Jews were to release their slaves, cancel all debts, and return land to the families of its original owners. While there is no record that the Jews ever kept that law, it became a symbol of the deliverance and new order of justice that God intended to bring about when he would right the wrongs suffered by his people (see Luke 1:51–55).

4:21 Today this scripture is fulfilled. Jesus asserts that the new era foretold by Isaiah has begun because he has come to bring it about. Isaiah's language regarding restored sight and release from slavery was figurative. Jesus' healings and exorcisms (which had made him so popular) were literal pointers to the truth that the new era of God's deliverance had begun and would come to pass through him.

4:22 All spoke well of him. The Greek word *martureo*, which is translated in the positive sense in this verse, can also be translated "to condemn" or "to speak against," depending on its context (com-

pare Acts 13:22 with Matt. 23:31)! The violent response later in this story (v. 28) shows that the final reaction toward Jesus was decidedly negative. Whether or not there was an initial positive reaction, the congregation quickly becomes shocked at the way Jesus is applying this passage to himself.

Joseph's son. This may be a slur, alluding to rumors of Jesus' illegitimacy (see also Mark 6:3). In stark contrast to God's declaration in Luke 3:22 (also Matt. 3:17) that Jesus is God's Son, the hometown people could only see Jesus as Joseph's boy. Who did this carpenter's son think he was anyway?

4:23 Physician, heal yourself. This proverb has both Greek and Arabic parallels. The doubt and cynicism of his hometown is seen in that they would not believe the stories they had heard elsewhere unless they could see further evidence. It is probable that the signs which Jesus had already given were not respected.

Capernaum. According to Mark's Gospel, this is the village in which Jesus first began to teach and heal (Mark 1:21ff).

4:24 no prophet is accepted in his hometown. This proverb (Mark 6:4; John 4:44) also has Greek parallels. It simply observes that the hardest place for a famous person to gain respect is among the people he or she grew up with. The irony is that while they will honor Isaiah as a prophet, they refuse to see the fulfillment of his word in Jesus.

4:25–27 While neither Elijah nor Elisha were rejected by their own people, their ministry extended to others outside of Israel as well. These stories, found in 1 Kings 17:1–18:2 and 2 Kings 5:1–27, illustrate that God has never limited his grace only to Israel. They further emphasize the point that if Nazareth (and, by extension, the Jews as a whole) will not receive Jesus with faith, then there are plenty of others (including Gentiles) who will. This was incendiary language!

4:28–29 Jesus' strong words, which implied that Gentiles were more worthy of God's grace than the people from Jesus' hometown, provoked such a strong response that a mob desired to kill him.

4:30 he walked right through the crowd. This illustrates the proper fulfillment of Psalm 91:11–12, which Satan had twisted in his temptation of Jesus (Luke 4:10–11; see notes on Matt. 4:6 in Unit 2). How Jesus did so is unclear.

UNIT 4—Calling of the First Disciples / John 1:35-51

Jesus' First Disciples

³⁵The next day John was there again with two of his disciples. ³⁶When he saw Jesus passing by, he said, "Look, the Lamb of God!"

³⁷When the two disciples heard him say this, they followed Jesus. ³⁸Turning around, Jesus saw them following and asked, "What do you want?"

They said, "Rabbi" (which means Teacher), "where are you staying?"

³⁹"Come," he replied, "and you will see."

So they went and saw where he was staying, and spent that day with him. It was about the tenth hour.

⁴⁰Andrew, Simon Peter's brother, was one of the two who heard what John had said and who had followed Jesus. ⁴¹The first thing Andrew did was to find his brother Simon and tell him, "We have found the Messiah" (that is, the Christ). ⁴²And he brought him to Jesus.

Jesus looked at him and said, "You are Simon son of John. You will be called Cephas" (which, when translated, is Peter).

Jesus Calls Philip and Nathanael

⁴³The next day Jesus decided to leave for Galilee. Finding Philip, he said to him, "Follow me."

⁴⁴Philip, like Andrew and Peter, was from the town of Bethsaida. ⁴⁵Philip found Nathanael and told him, "We have found the one Moses wrote about in the Law, and about whom the prophets also wrote—Jesus of Nazareth, the son of Joseph."

⁴⁶"Nazareth! Can anything good come from there?" Nathanael asked.

"Come and see," said Philip.

⁴⁷When Jesus saw Nathanael approaching, he said of him, "Here is a true Israelite, in whom there is nothing false."

⁴⁸"How do you know me?" Nathanael asked.

Jesus answered, "I saw you while you were still under the fig tree before Philip called you."

⁴⁹Then Nathanael declared, "Rabbi, you are the Son of God; you are the King of Israel."

⁵⁰Jesus said, "You believe because I told you I saw you under the fig tree. You shall see greater things than that." ⁵¹He then added, "I tell you the truth, you shall see heaven open, and the angels of God ascending and descending on the Son of Man."

READ

First Reading / First Impressions: What is your immediate reaction to this passage?

❐ Why are these incidents in the Bible? ❐ Who are these guys?

❐ This is a funny way to go about picking a team. ❐ other:_____

❐ Jesus should have been more careful about picking his team.

Second Reading / Big Idea: None of the other Gospels include these stories. Why do you think John included them?

SEARCH

1. In the dialogue between two of John the Baptist's disciples and Jesus (vv. 37–39), what was the double meaning of Jesus' invitation, "Come, and you will see" (see note on v. 39)?

2. Why did each of these men decide to follow Jesus?

Andrew:

Simon Peter:

Philip:

Nathanael:

3. What titles are used by each of the following people to describe Jesus, and what is the significance of each title (see notes)?

John the Baptist (v. 36):

John's disciples (v. 38):

Andrew (v. 41):

Nathanael (v. 49):

Jesus (of himself) (v. 51):

4. What do you learn about the nature and character of Jesus from this passage?

APPLY

1. In comparison to these disciples, what first drew you to follow Jesus?

2. When it comes to Jesus' invitation to "come and see," I am:
   ❏ still checking out Jesus on the basis of someone else's recommendation
   ❏ going after him to get to know him myself
   ❏ eager to invite others to join me in my journey with Jesus
   ❏ skeptical that there really is anything to this business
   ❏ overwhelmed with the insight Jesus has of me

3. Today, how would you characterize your follow-through on your call to be a disciple?
   ❏ Jesus is my Lord, and I follow him daily.
   ❏ Jesus is a great rabbi; I listen, but follow when I like.
   ❏ Jesus is my Savior, but we don't have a close relationship.
   ❏ Jesus is the Son of God, but not too involved in my daily life.
   ❏ Jesus is my Messiah, and I'm here to find out what that means.

4. What is one thing that would help you improve your follow-through in being a disciple?

GROUP AGENDA

After the first part, read the Scripture out loud and divide into groups of 4. Then come back together for the third part.

TO BEGIN / 10–15 Min. (Choose 1 or 2)

1. As a kid, how willing were you to believe anything your brother or sister told you?

2. What person saw some potential in you when you did not see it yourself?

3. When you get some good news, who are the first two people you want to share it with?

TO GO DEEPER / 30 Min. (Choose 2 or 3)

1. In light of the homework, what stands out to you about these stories of Jesus calling the first disciples?

2. Do you think Jesus took a chance by inviting these people to be on his team—or did he know beforehand that they would all be winners?

3. Which title or description of Jesus in this passage seems particularly significant or meaningful?

4. If you had to point to a time in your life when Jesus became more than just a name to you, what would you say? Who was the Andrew or Philip who first challenged you to consider following Jesus?

5. Who is the Peter or Nathanael you hope to introduce to Jesus?

6. CASE STUDY: Stewart was sexually abused as a child. He got into drugs as a teenager, was convicted and served time for assaulting a police officer. When the pastor appealed for someone to head up a program for abused children, he was the only person to volunteer. What should the leaders of the church do?

TO CLOSE / 15–30 Min.

1. Has your group taken the survey for small groups in your church (see page M15 in the center section)? If so, what are you going to do as a result?

2. Share your answer to one or two of the questions in APPLY.

3. How can your fellow disciples pray for you?

NOTES

Summary. Jesus did not conduct his ministry all alone. He called 12 men to be his close companions. Others also became his disciples—for example, the 72 he sent out ahead of him to the towns and places he was planning to visit (Luke 10:1–12). Certain women became his disciples as well, which was amazing in a day when women were not taken seriously. In this passage, Jesus meets some of the men he will later call his disciples (see Mark 1:16–20; 3:13–19). At first glance, this passage seems to be full of rather insignificant conversations. But it is full of allusions to the meaning of discipleship and to the identity of Jesus. The identity of Jesus is progressively revealed through a series of titles. He is called the Lamb of God (v. 36); Rabbi (vv. 38,49); the Messiah (v. 41); the Son of God (v. 49); the King of Israel (v. 49); and the Son of Man (v. 51). The other Gospels make it clear Jesus' true identity was not recognized early in his ministry. This points out that the author's intention here is not so much to give a chronological account of Jesus' first days of ministry, but to declare clearly Jesus' identity to his readers right from the beginning. The rest of the Gospel provides evidence through Jesus' miracles and his teachings as to why these titles are appropriate.

1:35 _John was there again._ This refers to John the Baptist, who was baptizing "at Bethany on the other side of the Jordan" (John 1:28).

two of his disciples. A disciple was simply a person who adhered to the teachings of a particular rabbi or inspired teacher. John the Baptist had enormous popular appeal, and had gathered many disciples from as far away as Alexandria in Egypt to Ephesus in present-day Turkey (Acts 18:24–19:3).

1:36 _the Lamb of God._ Raymond Brown notes that the author may intend two possible allusions: (1) To the Passover ritual, in which a lamb was killed so the wrath of God would "pass over" the home of the Israelites in Egypt (Ex. 12:1–23); or (2) To Isaiah's Suffering Servant "led like a lamb to the slaughter" (Isa. 53:7) as he "took up our infirmities" (Isa. 53:4).

1:38 _Rabbi._ Rabbis were teachers who gathered disciples around them. This is the recognition of Jesus' teaching authority.

1:39 _Come ... and you will see._ John's Gospel is fond of language that has double meanings. On the one hand, this appears to be a simple invitation to accompany Jesus to his residence. On the other hand, by this statement, Jesus invites these followers to enter into the journey of discipleship with him. Only as they commit themselves to follow him will they perceive the nature of his true home and identity.

1:41 *Andrew / Simon.* Although the implication is that all of this happens in Judea near the Jordan River (see v. 43), there is no record in the other Gospels that Jesus first met Simon Peter outside of Galilee. His presence in Judea in this Gospel suggests that Peter may have been a follower of John the Baptist as well (or at least someone who traveled to Judea in order to be baptized by John as a sign of his repentance). It is probable that the disciples' decision to follow Jesus actually was the result of several encounters that led them to the conclusion that he was one in whom they wished to invest their lives (see Mark 1:16–20).

We have found the Messiah. The Messiah was the one the people of Israel expected would be sent from God to deliver them from their oppression by Rome and restore Israel to its former greatness as a nation. He would be like the ancient King David, a powerful king who would rally his people together in a fight for freedom. Jesus poured a new meaning into this word. He taught that the deliverance he came to bring was a deliverance from sin that would usher in the kingdom of God.

that is, the Christ. This parenthetical expression is the author's commentary to his readers as he translates the Hebrew term "Messiah" into its Greek equivalent "Christ."

1:42 *Cephas.* The Aramaic name Cephas and the Greek name Peter both mean "rock." Although Peter sometimes seemed inconsistent and uncertain during Jesus' time with him (John 18:15–17,25–27), Peter became the chief spokesman for the apostles after Jesus returned to heaven and the Holy Spirit came at Pentecost (Acts 2:14). The implication is that the decision to come to Jesus is one that will change a person from the inside out, producing a new character.

1:43–44 *Galilee ... Bethsaida.* So far the story has centered in Judea. Galilee, where Jesus spent his boyhood, was a province 60 miles north of Jerusalem. Bethsaida was a village on the Sea of Galilee.

1:45 *Nathanael.* Like Andrew, Philip's response to discovering Jesus was to tell someone else. While Philip is found in the list of apostles mentioned in the other Gospels, Nathanael is not. It may be that he also bore the name Bartholomew, since in the other Gospels Philip and Bartholomew are mentioned together (i.e., Mark 3:18). It is also possible that he may not have been one of the apostles at all.

about whom the prophets also wrote. This refers to the common OT expectation that God would send a leader who would save his people (i.e., Isa. 11:1–9; Micah 5:2).

1:46 *Nazareth!* Nazareth was a small, insignificant village in Galilee. Undoubtedly, it seemed impossible to Nathanael that anyone important could come from there.

1:47 *a true Israelite.* Jesus' greeting implies an awareness of Nathanael's spiritual motivations reflected in that Nathanael, unlike Israel as a whole, came to Jesus. Israel was to be a people prepared to respond to God, but for the most part the nation failed to reflect that purpose.

in whom there is nothing false. This was not flattery, nor blindness to the fact that Nathanael had faults. Rather, it is a statement affirming Nathanael's sincerity and openness to God.

1:48 *I saw you.* This accents the supernatural knowledge of Jesus.

1:49 *Son of God.* This is a royal title used in the OT to refer to Israel's kings who were called God's "Sons." Jesus, by virtue of his existence before creation and his identity with God (John 1:1–2), is God's Son in a unique sense.

King of Israel. God was always considered the real King of Israel (Ps. 95:3; Isa. 44:6). Jesus has come to lead Israel to the fulfillment of God's plans for the people.

1:51 This recalls Jacob's dream (Gen. 28:10–12), with the significant difference that Jesus replaces the ladder as the means of communication between heaven and earth.

you. This is a plural term referring to all who believe, not just Nathanael.

the Son of Man. Of all the titles for Jesus in this chapter, this is the one Jesus uses of himself. Daniel 7:13ff provides for its background. The Son of Man is the One invested with divine authority to rule the earth, but it was not a commonly used term for the Messiah in Jesus' time. He may have used it precisely because it did not invoke the narrowly nationalistic stereotypes of the Messiah.

Feb 6, 2000

UNIT 5—Clashes With Religious Leaders / Mark 2:13-22; 3:1-6

The Calling of Levi

¹³*Once again Jesus went out beside the lake. A large crowd came to him, and he began to teach them.* ¹⁴*As he walked along, he saw Levi son of Alphaeus sitting at the tax collector's booth. "Follow me," Jesus told him, and Levi got up and followed him.*

¹⁵*While Jesus was having dinner at Levi's house, many tax collectors and "sinners" were eating with him and his disciples, for there were many who followed him.* ¹⁶*When the teachers of the law who were Pharisees saw him eating with the "sinners" and tax collectors, they asked his disciples: "Why does he eat with tax collectors and 'sinners'?"*

¹⁷*On hearing this, Jesus said to them, "It is not the healthy who need a doctor, but the sick. I have not come to call the righteous, but sinners."*

Jesus Questioned About Fasting

¹⁸*Now John's disciples and the Pharisees were fasting. Some people came and asked Jesus, "How is it that John's disciples and the disciples of the Pharisees are fasting, but yours are not?"*

¹⁹*Jesus answered, "How can the guests of the bridegroom fast while he is with them? They can-not, so long as they have him with them.* ²⁰*But the time will come when the bridegroom will be taken from them, and on that day they will fast.*

²¹*"No one sews a patch of unshrunk cloth on an old garment. If he does, the new piece will pull away from the old, making the tear worse.* ²²*And no one pours new wine into old wineskins. If he does, the wine will burst the skins, and both the wine and the wineskins will be ruined. No, he pours new wine into new wineskins." ...*

3 *Another time he went into the synagogue, and a man with a shriveled hand was there.* ²*Some of them were looking for a reason to accuse Jesus, so they watched him closely to see if he would heal him on the Sabbath.* ³*Jesus said to the man with the shriveled hand, "Stand up in front of everyone."*

⁴*Then Jesus asked them, "Which is lawful on the Sabbath: to do good or to do evil, to save life or to kill?" But they remained silent.*

⁵*He looked around at them in anger and, deeply distressed at their stubborn hearts, said to the man, "Stretch out your hand." He stretched it out, and his hand was completely restored.* ⁶*Then the Pharisees went out and began to plot with the Herodians how they might kill Jesus.*

READ

First Reading / First Impressions: If you were going to feature these stories on the evening news, how would you promote them?

❒ Rabbi defends eating habits.

❒ New rules for new rabbi.

❒ A rabbi who prefers to be with sinners!

❒ Teacher defies Pharisees with Sabbath miracle.

❒ Rabbi orders new wineskins.

❒ Rabbi says, "Eat, drink and be merry!"

❒ No "fast track" for Jesus!

❒ other:_____

Second Reading / Big Idea: How convincing do you think Jesus' actions and replies were to the people who questioned him?

❒ very   ❒ somewhat   ❒ a little   ❒ not at all

SEARCH

1. Read the notes for 2:14. How do you suppose the disciples felt when Jesus asked Matthew (Levi) to join the group? How do you imagine Matthew felt?

Disciples	Matthew

2. What does Jesus mean when he says to the Pharisees, "It is not the healthy who need a doctor, but the sick. I have not come to call the righteous, but sinners" (v. 17; see note)?

3. Why, according to Jesus, didn't his disciples fast (v. 19)? When would they (v. 20)?

4. What is the point of the two parables in 2:21–22 (see note)?

5. What causes the tension in the synagogue (3:1–6)? What emotions does this scene stir within Jesus?

6. Why would the Pharisees scheme with the Herodians—whom they normally despised (3:6; see note)? Ironically, how were they in reality responding to Jesus' question in 3:4?

APPLY

1. How in touch are you with the "tax collectors" and "sinners" of your community? (Place an *"X"* on the line where you see yourself.)

standing outside	**in the same house**	**in the same room**	**at the same table**

2. How has (or should) Jesus' "new wine" burst some of your "old wineskins"—your religious rituals and ruts?

GROUP AGENDA

After the first part, read the Scripture out loud and divide into groups of 4. Then come back together for the third part.

TO BEGIN / 10–15 Min. (Choose 1 or 2)

1. Have you ever been in a situation in which you felt totally out of place? How did you handle it?

2. Which of your parents' rules did you break most often?

3. What Sunday restrictions, if any, did you grow up with? Do you still honor them?

TO GO DEEPER / 30 Min. (Choose 2 or 3)

1. How could Jesus call Levi (or Matthew)—a person with a reputation as a traitor and a cheat—as a disciple? How do you feel about Jesus hanging out with tax collectors and "sinners"?

2. Based on this passage and the homework for it, why was there such intense conflict between Jesus and the religious leaders?

3. How have you seen religious rules or institutions hurt people? How might you be guilty of that yourself?

4. What can you do to reach out to "sinners"? How can you help ensure your church is more concerned with people's needs than rules and regulations?

5. CASE STUDY: At historic First Church (where many of the important people in town attend) the pastor decided to open the door to the "broken people" in the community by offering support groups for alcoholics, drug addicts, sex offenders and AIDS patients. Many people who have not attended church for many years (if ever) have started coming to church. What should the church do?

TO CLOSE / 15–30 Min.

1. Are you working on your mission as a group? Are you inviting new people to join you?

2. What did you learn about yourself in APPLY?

3. Is your spiritual life more like a new wineskin or a patch job of an old wineskin?

4. How can the group pray for you?

NOTES

Summary. In a previous unit we encountered the beginning of opposition to the ministry of Jesus. The reaction against him in Nazareth was unusual, however, since most people were quite enthusiastic about Jesus. His real opposition came from the religious leaders. In the three stories that follow, we see them probe Jesus ("Is he one of us?"), question Jesus ("Does he abide by our unwritten laws?"), and then come to the awful conclusion that not only is Jesus dangerous, he needs to be killed (Mark 3:6). In this unit, we will study three stories that Mark tells in order to show the nature of (and reason for) the opposition by the religious leaders. They are set in contrast to a previous series of stories (Mark 1:16–45) that show how popular Jesus was with the common people. News about Jesus has spread everywhere (Mark 1:28,45). It is not surprising, therefore, that the religious leaders want to know who he is and what he stands for.

2:13–17 In this story, the religious leaders question Jesus about his adherence to ritual law (in this case, eating with those who are considered "unclean"). In this story Jesus also chooses another disciple.

2:14 *Levi.* Elsewhere he is identified as Matthew (Matt. 9:9), the disciple who eventually wrote one of the Gospels. By all counts Matthew was a poor candidate for a disciple. In his role as tax collector, he was hated by both the religious establishment and the common people.

tax collector's booth. Considered as vile as robbers or murderers, tax collectors in Galilee were seen by their fellow Jews as traitors, because they collaborated with the Roman power in order to become wealthy. Since only the tax collector knew the tax rate required by Rome, he was free to charge whatever the market would bear. Once he paid what he owed Rome, the rest was his to keep. A major international road ran through Capernaum. Matthew's job may have been to collect the tolls from the caravans that used the road, or to collect duties on goods shipped across the lake.

Follow me. In Matthew, Mark and Luke, this is the key phrase regarding discipleship. Only those who leave their past behind to follow Jesus in faith and obedience are his disciples. While we are not told what else transpired that moved Matthew to respond this way, the crucial point is that he did choose to turn away from his past loyalties to pursue the way of Jesus.

2:15 *having dinner.* To share a meal with another was a significant event, implying acceptance of that person. In this way, Jesus extends his forgiveness to those who were seen as standing outside orthodox religious life.

"*sinners.*" This was a slang phrase for those who failed to observe religious practices. These were generally the common people who had to work for a living and thus did not have enough time to keep all the ritual law (e.g., they did not wash their hands in a special, complicated way before a meal). Since these particular "sinners" associated with tax collectors, it is likely that they, too, were cut off from "proper" society.

2:16 *Pharisees.* This was a small but powerful religious sect (about 6,000 members at the time of Herod). The group's prime concern was knowing and keeping the Law in all its detail. In their sincere effort to do this, Pharisees often became rigid, censorious and deaf to the voice of God.

Why does he eat ...? They could not understand how a truly religious person could eat with people whose moral life was disreputable and who ate food that was prepared and served in ways that violated the practices regarding ritual cleanliness.

2:17 Jesus responds by way of a metaphor laced with irony. At first glance, the Pharisees would perhaps have considered this a reasonable explanation of his behavior: he came to heal those who were sick—which to them meant the "sinners" with whom he ate. In later reflection they might come to wonder if perhaps Jesus considered them the sick ones!

2:18–22 The next question has to do with ritual law—in this case, the issue of fasting.

2:18 *John's disciples.* These are followers of John the Baptist.

fasting. Although the OT Law did not require it, the Pharisees did not eat from 6 a.m. to 6 p.m. on Mondays and Thursdays as an act of piety. Regular fasting was assumed to be part of any serious religious discipline. The implication of the question is that there is something deficient about Jesus' disciples, because they do not observe rituals of fasting.

2:19–20 Jesus uses a brief parable to make his point. It would be entirely inappropriate for wedding guests to mourn when the groom appears! For the really poor there were few events to break the monotony and tedium of their lives. Marriage was one such occasion. Rather than go on a honeymoon, a Jewish couple stayed with their friends for a week-long feast during which everyone was released from all religious obligations, including fasting. Jesus implies that fasting (a sign of mourning) is inappropriate because he is on the scene. This enigmatic parable is loaded with implications, since God, in the OT, is often referred to as the bridegroom of Israel.

2:20 *the bridegroom will be taken from them.* This ominous note, which does not fit with anyone's common ideas about what happens at a wedding, foreshadows Jesus' death. It will be as if the groom is suddenly, violently abducted just prior to his wedding.

2:21–22 Jesus uses two more mini-parables to emphasize his point. A piece of unshrunk cloth sewn to an old garment will pull apart when washed. New wine as it ferments and expands will burst old, inflexible wineskins. Likewise, Jesus' new way is not compatible with the traditions and rituals of the Pharisees. His way differs from theirs not only in degree, but in kind.

3:1–6 In the final incident in these five confrontation stories (Mark 2:1–3:6), the religious leaders come to a conclusion about Jesus: he is dangerous and so must die.

3:2 *they watched him closely.* By this time the religious leaders no longer questioned Jesus. Now they simply watched to see if his actions showed a disregard for law.

if he would heal on the Sabbath. The issue is not healing, but whether Jesus would heal on the Sabbath in defiance of the oral tradition of the rabbis (which allowed healing only if there was danger to life). Jesus could have waited until the next day to heal this long-paralyzed hand.

3:5 *anger / deeply distressed.* Once again, Mark identifies the emotions of Jesus (see Mark 1:41). Jesus felt strongly about the injustice of a system that sacrificed the genuine needs of people for the traditions of men—all in the name of piety.

3:6 *Herodians.* A political group made up of influential Jewish sympathizers of King Herod. They were normally despised by the Pharisees, who considered them traitors (for working with Rome) and irreligious (i.e., unclean). However, the Pharisees have no power to kill Jesus. This must come from civil authority, and hence the collaboration.

UNIT 6—Healing Sick, Blind & Demon-Possessed / Matt. 9:18-34

A Dead Girl and a Sick Woman

¹⁸*While he was saying this, a ruler came and knelt before him and said, "My daughter has just died. But come and put your hand on her, and she will live."* ¹⁹*Jesus got up and went with him, and so did his disciples.*

²⁰*Just then a woman who had been subject to bleeding for twelve years came up behind him and touched the edge of his cloak.* ²¹*She said to herself, "If I only touch his cloak, I will be healed."*

²²*Jesus turned and saw her. "Take heart, daughter," he said, "your faith has healed you." And the woman was healed from that moment.*

²³*When Jesus entered the ruler's house and saw the flute players and the noisy crowd,* ²⁴*he said, "Go away. The girl is not dead but asleep." But they laughed at him.* ²⁵*After the crowd had been put outside, he went in and took the girl by the hand, and she got up.* ²⁶*News of this spread through all that region.*

Jesus Heals the Blind and Mute

²⁷*As Jesus went on from there, two blind men followed him, calling out, "Have mercy on us, Son of David!"*

²⁸*When he had gone indoors, the blind men came to him, and he asked them, "Do you believe that I am able to do this?"*

"Yes, Lord," they replied.

²⁹*Then he touched their eyes and said, "According to your faith will it be done to you";* ³⁰*and their sight was restored. Jesus warned them sternly, "See that no one knows about this."* ³¹*But they went out and spread the news about him all over that region.*

³²*While they were going out, a man who was demon-possessed and could not talk was brought to Jesus.* ³³*And when the demon was driven out, the man who had been mute spoke. The crowd was amazed and said, "Nothing like this has ever been seen in Israel."*

³⁴*But the Pharisees said, "It is by the prince of demons that he drives out demons."*

READ

First Reading / First Impressions: What would you write as your newspaper headline if you were reporting on these events?

Second Reading / Big Idea: How would the community where you live be affected if four miracles like this happened in one day?

SEARCH

1. What four types of people came to Jesus asking for help, and what were their needs (see notes)?

	Type	Need
a.		
b.		
c.		
d.		

Leadership Training Supplement

YOU ARE
HERE

BIRTH   GROWTH   RELEASE

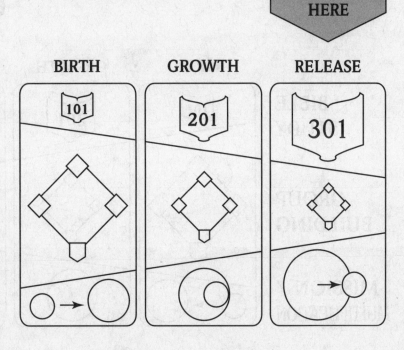

101   201   301

What is the game plan for your group in the 301 stage?

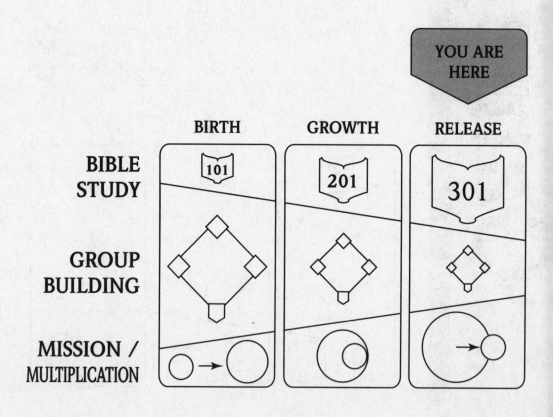

YOU ARE HERE

	BIRTH	GROWTH	RELEASE
BIBLE STUDY	101	201	301
GROUP BUILDING			
MISSION / MULTIPLICATION			

The three essentials in a healthy small group are Bible Study, Group Building, and Mission / Multiplication. You need all three to stay balanced—like a 3-legged stool.
- To focus only on Bible Study will lead to scholasticism.
- To focus only on Group Building will lead to narcissism.
- To focus only on Mission will lead to burnout.

You need a game plan for the life cycle of the group where all of these elements are present in a purpose-driven strategy.

e 3-Legged Stool

Bible Study

To develop the habit and skills for personal Bible Study.

TWO LEVELS: (1) Personal—on your own, and (2) Group study with your small group. In the personal Bible Study, you will be introduced to skills for reflection, self-inventory, creative writing and journaling.

Group Building

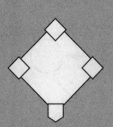

To move into discipleship with group accountability, shared leadership and depth community.

At the close of this course, the group building aspect will reach its goal with a "going-away" party. If there are other groups in the church in this program, the event would be for all groups. Otherwise, the group will have its own closing celebration and commissioning time.

Mission / Multiplication

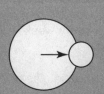

To commission the members of the leadership team from your group who are going to start a new group.

This Leadership Training Supplement is about your mission project. In six steps, your group will be led through a decision-making process to discover the leadership team within your group to form a new group.

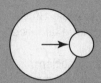

Mission / Multiplication

Where are you in the 3-stage life cycle of your mission?

You can't sit on a one-legged stool—or even a two-legged stool. It takes all three. A Bible Study and Care Group that doesn't have a MISSION will fall.

Birthing Cycle

The mission is to give birth to a new group at the conclusion of this course. In this 301 course, you are supposed to be at stage three. If you are not at stage three, you can still reach the mission goal if you stay focused.

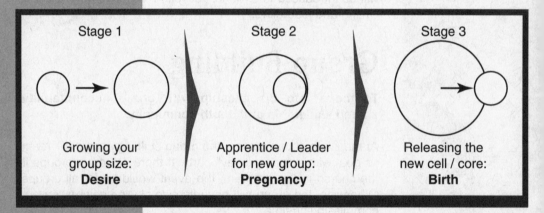

Stage 1	Stage 2	Stage 3
Growing your group size: **Desire**	Apprentice / Leader for new group: **Pregnancy**	Releasing the new cell / core: **Birth**

The birthing process begins with DESIRE. If you do not want to birth a new group, it will never happen. Desire keeps the group focused on inviting new people into your group every week—until your group grows to about 10 or 12 people.

The second stage is PREGNANCY. By recognizing the gifts of people in your group, you are able to designate two or three people who will ultimately be the missionaries in your group to form a new group. This is called the "leadership core."

The third stage is BIRTH—which takes place at the end of this course, when the whole group commissions the core or cell to move out and start the new group.

6 Steps to Birth a Group

Step 1

Desire

Is your group purpose-driven about mission?

Take this pop quiz and see how purpose-driven you are. Then, study the "four fallacies" about groups.

Step 2

Assessment

Is your church purpose-driven about groups?

Pinpoint where you are coming from and where most of the people in small groups in your church come from.

Step 3

Survey

Where's the itch for those in your church who are not involved in groups?

Take this churchwide survey to discover the felt needs of those in your church who do not seem to be interested in small groups.

Step 4

Brainstorming

What did you learn about your church from the survey?

Debrief the survey in the previous step to decide how your small group could make a difference in starting a new group.

Step 5

Barnstorming

Who are you going to invite?

Build a prospect list of people you think might be interested in joining a new group.

Step 6

Commissioning

Congratulations. You deserve a party.

Commission the leadership core from your group who are going to be your missionaries to start a new group. Then, for the rest of the "mother group," work on your covenant for starting over ... with a few empty chairs.

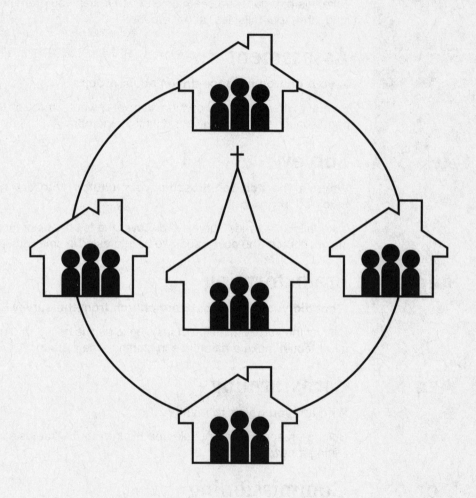

Step 1

Desire

Is your group purpose-driven about mission?

The greatest danger to any chain is its strongest link. This is especially true of Bible Study groups. The very depth of the study keeps new people from joining, or feeling comfortable when they join. In the end the group grows inward, becoming self-centered and spiritually insensitive.

To prevent this from happening in your group, take this pop quiz and share the results with your group.

	Yes	No
1. Are you a committed follower of Jesus Christ?	☐	☐
2. Do you believe that Jesus Christ wants you to share your faith with others?	☐	☐
3. Do you believe that every Christian needs to belong to a small, caring community where Jesus Christ is affirmed?	☐	☐
4. Do you know of people in your church who are not presently involved in a small group?	☐	☐
5. Do you know friends on the fringe of the church who need to belong to a life-sharing small group?	☐	☐
6. Do you believe that God has a will and plan for your life?	☐	☐
7. Are you willing to be open to what God might do through you in this small group?	☐	☐
8. Are you open to the possibility that God might use you to form a new group?	☐	☐

If you can't say "No" to any of these questions, consider yourself committed!

What Is a Small Group?

A Small Group is an intentional, face-to-face gathering of people in a similar stage of life at a regular time with a common purpose of discovering and growing in a relationship with Jesus Christ.

Small Groups are the disciple-making strategy of Flamingo Road Church. The behaviors of the 12 step strategy are the goals we want to achieve with each individual in small group. These goals are accomplished through a new members class (membership) and continues in a regular on-going small group (maturity, ministry and multiplication).

Keys to an Effective Small Group Ministry

1. Care for all people (members/guests) through organized active Care Groups.
2. Teach the Bible interactively while making life application.
3. Build a Servant Leadership Team.
4. Birth New Groups.

Commitments of all Small Group Leaders are ...

... all the behaviors represented in the 12 step strategy
... to lead their group to be an effective small group as mentioned above.
... use curriculum approved by small group pastor

Taken from the Small Group Training Manual of Flamingo Road Community Church, Fort Lauderdale, FL.

Four Fallacies About Small Groups

Are you suffering from one of these four misconceptions when it comes to small groups? Check yourself on these fallacies.

Fallacy #1: It takes 10 to 12 people to start a small group.

Wrong. The best size to start with is three or four people—which leaves room in the group for growth. Start "small" and pray that God will fill the "empty chair" ... and watch it happen.

Fallacy #2: It takes a lot of skill to lead a small group.

Wrong again. Sticking to the three-part tight agenda makes it possible for nearly anyone to lead a group. For certain support and recovery groups more skills are required, but the typical Bible Study and Care Group can be led by anyone with lots of heart and vision.

Fallacy #3: To assure confidentiality, the "door" should be closed after the first session.

For certain "high risk" groups this is true; but for the average Bible Study and Care Group all you need is the rule that "nothing that is said in the group is discussed outside of the group."

Fallacy #4: The longer the group lasts, the better it gets.

Not necessarily. The bell curve for effective small groups usually peaks in the second year. Unless new life is brought into the group, the group will decline in vitality. It is better to release the group (and become a reunion group) when it is at its peak than to run the risk of burnout.

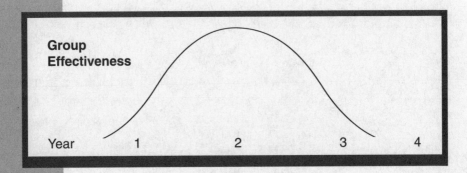

Group
Effectiveness

Year   1   2   3   4

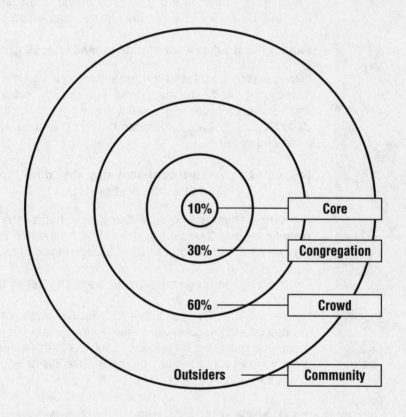

Step 2

Assessment

Is your church purpose-driven about groups?

Most of the people who come to small groups in the church are from the highly committed CORE of the church. How about your group?

Pinpoint Your Group

The graph on the opposite page represents the four types of people typically found in your church and in your community.

- **10% Core:** The "spiritual core" of the church and the church leadership.

- **30% Congregation:** Those who come to church regularly and are faithful in giving.

- **60% Crowd:** Those on the membership roles who attend only twice a year. They have fallen through the cracks.

- **Outside Community:** Those who live in the surrounding area but do not belong to any church.

Step 1: On the opposite page, put a series of dots in the appropriate circles where the members of your group come from.

Step 2: If you know of other small groups in your church, put some more dots on the graph to represent the people in those groups. When you are finished, stop and ask your group this question:

"Why do the groups in our church appeal only to the people who are represented by the dots on this graph?"

Four Kinds of Small Groups

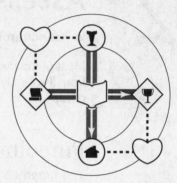

SUPPORT / RECOVERY GROUPS
- Felt needs
- Short-term
- Low-level commitment
- Seeker Bible Study

These groups are designed to appeal to hurting people on the fringe of the church and in the community.

PULPIT-BASED GROUPS
- Around the Scripture in the Sunday lesson
- With handout in Sunday bulletin
- With discussion questions
- No homework

These groups are designed to appeal to those who come to church and listen to the sermon but do not want to do homework.

DISCIPLESHIP / DEPTH BIBLE STUDY GROUPS
- Year-long commitment
- Depth Bible Study
- Homework required
- Curriculum based

These groups are designed to appeal to the 10% highly committed core of the church who are ready for discipleship.

COVENANT GROUPS
- Three-stage life cycle
- Renewal option
- Begins with 7-week contract
- Graded levels of Bible Study: 101, 201 and 301

Church Evaluation

You do NOT have to complete this assessment if you are not in the leadership core of your church, but it would be extremely valuable if your group does have members in the leadership core of your church.

1. Currently, what percentage of your church members are involved in small groups?

2. What kind of small groups are you offering in your church? (Study the four kinds of groups on the opposite page.)
   ❏ Support / Recovery Groups
   ❏ Pulpit-Based Groups
   ❏ Discipleship / Depth Bible Study Groups
   ❏ Three-stage Covenant Groups

3. Which statement below represents the position of your church on small groups?
   ❏ "Small Groups have never been on the drawing board at our church."
   ❏ "We have had small groups, but they fizzled."
   ❏ "Our church leadership has had negative experiences with small groups."
   ❏ "Small groups are the hope for our future."
   ❏ "We have Sunday school; that's plenty."

4. How would you describe the people who usually get involved in small groups?
   ❏ 10% Core   ❏ 30% Congregation   ❏ 60% Crowd

Risk and Supervision
This depends on the risk level of the group—the higher the risk, the higher the supervision. For the typical Bible Study group ▢, pulpit-based group ⓨ, or covenant group ◈ (where there is little risk), supervision is minimal. For some support groups ♡ and all recovery groups ⚡, training and supervision are required.

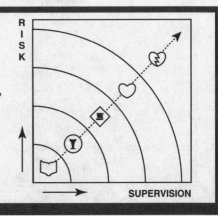

Step 3 Survey

Where's the itch for those in your church who are not involved in groups?

This survey has been written for churchwide use—in hopes that you may be able to rewrite it and use it in your own church. The courses described in this survey are taken from the present Serendipity 101, 201 and 301 courses for small groups.

Churchwide Survey for Small Groups

Name_____Phone_____

Section 1: Interest in Shared-Experience Groups

A shared-experience group is short-term in nature (7–13 weeks) and brings people together based on a common interest, experience or need in their lives. The various topics being considered for shared-experience groups are listed below.

1. Which of these shared-experience courses might be of interest to you? Check all that apply in the grid below under question 1 (**Q1**).

2. Which of these shared-experience groups would you be interested in hosting or co-leading? Check all that apply in the grid below under question 2 (**Q2**).

3. Which of these shared-experience groups do you think would be of interest to a friend or relative of yours who is on the fringe of the church? Check all that apply in the grid below under question 3 (**Q3**).

101 VIDEO Electives — 7–13 weeks: Sunday School with Groups

	Q1	Q2	Q3
1. Dealing With Grief & Loss (Hope in the Midst of Pain)	☐	☐	☐
2. Divorce Recovery (Picking Up the Pieces)	☐	☐	☐
3. Marriage Enrichment (Making a Good Marriage Better)	☐	☐	☐
4. Parenting Adolescents (Easing the Way to Adulthood)	☐	☐	☐
5. Healthy Relationships (Living Within Defined Boundaries)	☐	☐	☐
6. Stress Management (Finding the Balance)	☐	☐	☐
7. 12 Steps (The Path to Wholeness)	☐	☐	☐

Survey The Needs —

101 BEGINNER Bible Study — 7- to 13-week groups

	Q1	Q2	Q3
8. Stressed Out (Keeping Your Cool)	☐	☐	☐
9. Core Values (Setting My Moral Compass)	☐	☐	☐
10. Marriage (Seasons of Growth)	☐	☐	☐
11. Jesus (Up Close & Personal)	☐	☐	☐
12. Gifts & Calling (Discovering God's Will)	☐	☐	☐
13. Relationships (Learning to Love)	☐	☐	☐
14. Assessment (Personal Audit)	☐	☐	☐
15. Family (Stages of Parenting)	☐	☐	☐
16. Wholeness (Time for a Checkup)	☐	☐	☐
17. Beliefs (Basic Christianity)	☐	☐	☐

201 DEEPER Bible Study — Varying Length Courses

	Q1	Q2	Q3
18. Supernatural: Amazing Stories (Jesus' Miracles) 13 wks.	☐	☐	☐
19. Discipleship: In His Steps (Life of Christ) 13 wks.	☐	☐	☐
20. Wisdom: The Jesus Classics (Jesus' Parables) 13 wks.	☐	☐	☐
21. Challenge: Attitude Adjustment (Sermon on the Mount) 13 wks.	☐	☐	☐
22. Endurance: Running the Race (Philippians) 11 wks.	☐	☐	☐
23. Teamwork: Together in Christ (Ephesians) 12 wks.	☐	☐	☐
24. Integrity: Taking on Tough Issues (1 Corinthians) 12–23 wks.	☐	☐	☐
25. Gospel: Jesus of Nazareth (Gospel of Mark) 13–26 wks.	☐	☐	☐
26. Leadership: Passing the Torch (1 & 2 Timothy) 14 wks.	☐	☐	☐
27. Excellence: Mastering the Basics (Romans) 15–27 wks.	☐	☐	☐
28. Hope: Looking at the End of Time (Revelation) 13–26 wks.	☐	☐	☐
29. Faithfulness: Walking in the Light (1 John) 11 wks.	☐	☐	☐
30. Freedom: Living by Grace (Galatians) 13 wks.	☐	☐	☐
31. Perseverance: Staying the Course (1 Peter) 10 wks.	☐	☐	☐
32. Performance: Faith at Work (James) 12 wks.	☐	☐	☐

301 DEPTH Bible Study — 13-week groups

	Q1	Q2	Q3
33. Ephesians (Our Riches in Christ)	☐	☐	☐
34. James (Walking the Talk)	☐	☐	☐
35. Life of Christ (Behold the Man)	☐	☐	☐
36. Miracles (Signs and Wonders)	☐	☐	☐
37. Parables (Virtual Reality)	☐	☐	☐
38. Philippians (Joy Under Stress)	☐	☐	☐
39. Sermon on the Mount (Examining Your Life)	☐	☐	☐
40. 1 John (The Test of Faith)	☐	☐	☐

Section 2: Covenant Groups (Long-term)

A covenant group is longer term (like an extended family), starting with a commitment for 7–13 weeks, with an option of renewing your covenant for the rest of the year. A covenant group can decide to change the topics they study over time. The general themes for the covenant groups that our church is considering are listed on the previous two pages.

4. Which of the following long-term covenant groups would you be interested in?

❏ Singles	❏ Men	❏ Women
❏ Couples	❏ Parents	❏ Downtown
❏ Twenty-Something	❏ Thirty-Something	❏ Empty Nesters
❏ Mixed	❏ Breakfast	❏ Engineers
❏ Young Marrieds	❏ Seniors	❏ Sunday Brunch

Section 3: Pre-Covenant Groups (Short-term)

To give you a taste of a small group, our church is offering a 7-week "trial" program for groups. For this trial program, the group will use the course *Beginnings: A Taste of Serendipity.*

5. Would you be interested in joining a "trial" group?

❏ Yes   ❏ No   ❏ Maybe

6. What would be the most convenient time and place for you to meet?

❏ Weekday morning	❏ At church
❏ Weekday evening	❏ In a home
❏ Saturday morning	
❏ Sunday after church	

7. What kind of group would you prefer?

❏ Men
❏ Women
❏ Singles
❏ Couples
❏ Mixed
❏ Parents
❏ Seniors
❏ Around my age
❏ Doesn't matter

SERENDIPITY

BEGINNINGS

A TASTE OF SERENDIPITY

7 Sessions To Become
A Great Small Group!

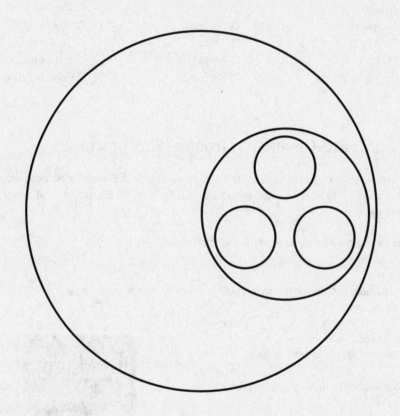

Step 4 Brainstorming

What did you learn about your church from the survey?

The Itch: Debrief together what you discovered from the survey about the need for small groups in your church. To begin with, find out in your group who checked Q3 for any of the 101 Video and 101 Beginner Electives (courses 1–17). Jot down in the box below the top three courses that you checked for 1–17.

Top Three Courses:

The Nitch: For the top three courses in the box above, find out if anyone in your group checked Q2 for these courses—i.e., that they would be willing to host or help lead a group that was interested in this course. Jot down the names of those in your group who checked Q2 in the box below.

Potential Hosts and Leaders:

The Apprentice / Leader and Leadership Core: Now, as a group, look over the names of the potential hosts and leaders you put in the box above and try to discern the person on this list who you think could easily be the leader of this new group, and one or two others who might fill out the Leadership Core for this new group. Jot down these names in the box below.

Apprentice / Leader and Leadership Core:

Q&A

What is the purpose of Covenant Groups?*

The members of the Covenant Group come together for the purpose of helping each other to:

- *Love God with all their heart, soul, mind and strength (Mark 12:30).*
- *Love their neighbors as themselves (Mark 12:31).*
- *Make disciples (Matthew 28:19).*

What are the qualifications of a Covenant Group leader?

A Covenant Group leader functions as a lay pastor, taking on himself or herself the responsibility of providing the primary care for the members of the group. Therefore, a Covenant Group leader exemplifies the following characteristics:

- *believes in Jesus Christ as their Lord and Savior*
- *has been a Christian for a while*
- *continues to grow in their faith*
- *cares for the well-being of others*
- *is able to set goals and work toward them*
- *demonstrates moral integrity*
- *listens to others*
- *is empathetic*
- *is willing to learn from others*
- *demonstrates flexibility*
- *respects others*
- *senses a call to serve*

A Covenant Group leader is not a perfect person! He or she need not know everything about leading and caring for others. Skills valuable to the role of a leader will be taught throughout the year, and care for the leader will be provided on an ongoing basis through a coach.

A Covenant Group leader is not necessarily a teacher. It is far more important that the leader be able to shepherd and care for the others in the group. Teaching is often a shared responsibility among group members.

---

* These four pages (M20–M23) are taken from the Training Manual For Group Leaders at Zionsville Presbyterian Church, Zionsville, IN, and are used by permission.

What does the church expect of a Covenant Group leader?

Every leader is asked to agree to the terms of the leader's covenant. Covenant Group leaders are to attend the monthly STP (Sharing, Training and Prayer) meeting. This gathering is held for the purposes of training and supporting leaders. The meeting takes place on the third Tuesday of each month, from 6:45 p.m. to 8:30 p.m. The two main elements of the STP event concern communication. The first half of the evening is devoted to disseminating the vision. The second half of the meeting consists of leaders huddling with their coach and with each other for the purpose of learning from one another. If a leader is unable to attend this meeting for some significant reason, he or she is to arrange another time to meet with their coach.

Leaders are also to fill out the Group Leader's Summary after every group event. This one-page reporting form takes only 10 minutes or so to complete and is a vital communication link between the staff liaison, the coach and the leader.

What can a Covenant Group leader expect in the way of support from the church?

A Covenant Group leader can expect the session and the staff to hold to the terms laid out in the Church's Covenant.

Every leader will be given a coach. This coach is someone whose ministry is to care for up to five leaders. The coach is charged with the responsibility of resourcing, encouraging, supporting, evaluating, challenging, loving and listening to the leaders in his or her care.

Every coach is supported by a staff member. If leaders ever have a situation where they feel that their coach is unable to help them, the staff liaison is there to be of assistance.

What is the role of a Covenant Group leader?

When people come together in groups, the group itself becomes an entity that is greater than the sum of its parts. The Covenant Group leader watches over the life and health of this new entity.

Specifically the Covenant Group leader is to:

- *find an apprentice*
- *pray and prepare for group meetings*
- *notify their coach or staff of acute crisis conditions requiring response*
- *develop and maintain an atmosphere in which members of the group can discover and develop God-given spiritual gifts*
- *pray for the spiritual growth and protection of each member*
- *refer counseling cases that exceed experience level*
- *convene the group two to four times each month*
- *recruit a host/hostess, when appropriate, and to see that child care and refreshments are available and a venue is arranged*
- *develop a healthy balance of love, learn, do, decide*
- *assure God's redemptive agenda via Scripture, sharing, prayers, songs and worship*
- *assist the group in refraining from divisiveness or teachings contrary to church position*
- *accept responsibility for group growth through the open-chair strategy*
- *lead an exemplary life*
- *regularly touch base with members outside the context of the group meeting just to say "Hi" and to see how they are doing*
- *help the group form a covenant and to review the covenant periodically*

While the Covenant Group leader takes primary responsibility for these activities, he or she should involve members of the group in many of them.

Does a Covenant Group really have to have a leader?

Yes! Without a leader a Covenant Group is like a ship at sea with no captain. A ship without a captain is at the mercy of the prevailing current and is unable to prepare for what may lie ahead. However, a ship with a captain has her course mapped out, and there is always someone at the helm ready to respond if necessary. So it is with a Covenant Group. The leader serves the others in the group by working to chart the best course as they together pursue being God's people on earth.

Questions & Answers

What are the critical elements of a Covenant Group?

A Covenant Group needs to have:

- *a leader*
- *an apprentice / leader*
- *members*

- *an open chair*
- *a covenant (see page M32)*

What is an Apprentice / Leader and how do we find one?

An apprentice / leader is someone who agrees that in time he or she will step out into leadership. Historically churches have tended to ask only those who aggressively step forward to serve in leadership positions. Rarely have churches worked at developing leaders. The result has been that most churches experience the phenomenon where only 20% of the congregation does 80% of the work. This historical approach stifles the giftedness of 80% of the church's population! In addition, the church has burned out many of their stand-out leaders by asking them to lead too many programs and too many people. Without some form of apprentice / leadership development, the church is constrained to overload its highly motivated, "here-I-am-send-me" leaders. The apprentice / leader model is meant to address these concerns.

The apprentice / leader is not an assistant. An assistant seldom has plans of stepping into the leader's shoes. Instead, the apprentice / leader works alongside the leader, with the intent of one day becoming a leader themselves. Along the way he or she is experiencing on-the-job training, learning the skills necessary to serve a small group as its leader.

It is the responsibility of the leader to find an apprentice / leader. The most important tools for the leader in this process are prayer and observation. The leader should pray, asking God to send someone whom he or she could mentor and train as a leader. Accompanying these prayers should be efforts to observe those who demonstrate signs of giftedness in shepherding, organizing, listening and faith. The one who is on time and who routinely prepares diligently for the group could be a candidate. The leader could also begin using the time before and after worship services, as well as various fellowship and educational events, to meet others in the congregation. As relationships are established, and the extent of a leader's acquaintances are broadened, the opportunity for finding a suitable apprentice / leader increases.

Step 5 Barnstorming

Who are you going to invite?

In the previous step, you identified the Apprentice / Leader and one or two others in your group who are going to be the leadership cell or core to start a new group.

Now, as a whole group, spend a few minutes creating a prospect list of people you would like to invite into this new group. Ask someone in your group to be the secretary and write down in the boxes below the names of people who come to mind:

Friends: Who are your friends in the church who you think might be interested in a small group?

```

```

Affinity: What are the special interests of the people in your leadership cell and who are the people in your church with the same interests? For instance, if the people in your leadership cell love tennis, who are the people in your church who might be interested in a small group before tennis? What about book lovers, entrepreneurs, empty nesters, senior citizens, stock watchers, etc.?

```

```

How Serendipity 101 Courses
Make Leading A Beginner Group Easy:

1. *Each session has get acquainted* **Ice-Breakers** *to get your group started and a* **3-Part Tight Agenda** *to keep it on track!*

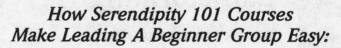

2. **Two Options** *for breaking open the Word:*
- **Option1: Light**—*for people who are not familiar with the Bible*
- **Option 2: Heavy**—*for people who are familiar with the Bible*

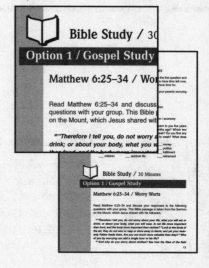

3. **Study Helps** *for the Group Leader include Margin Tips, Reference Notes and Guided Questionnaires for Bible Study.*

Who Do We Invite?

Felt Needs: Who are the people you know with the same felt needs? These people might be on the fringe of the church or even outside of the church. Go back to the survey on pages M15–M16 (the 101 courses) and think of people you feel could be hot prospects. For instance, who would be interested in "Stressed Out," "Marriage," "Wholeness," "Healthy Relationships," "Parenting Adolescents," etc.?

Geographical Location: Where do the people in your leadership team live or work, and who are the people in your church in the same area?

The Four Circles: Now, on this diagram, pinpoint the people you have jotted down in the four circles. Do you have any people on this list from the **Crowd** (the church dropouts)? Do you have anyone on your list from the **Community** (who do not attend any church)? It's really important that you have people from all four circles on your list.

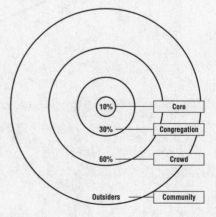

Step 6 Commissioning

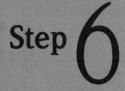

Congratulations. You deserve a party.

Only two things remain for you to decide: (1) How are you going to commission the leadership team for the new group and (2) What is the rest of your group going to do next?

Going-away party

You have several options. If the church is planning a church-wide event for all of the groups (such as a graduation banquet), you would have a table at this event for your group. If your church is not planning an event, you must plan your own going-away party.

At this party, you may want to reminisce about your life together as a group, have fun making some "Wild Predictions," share a Bible Study time, and conclude with a time of commissioning and prayer.

Reminiscing Questions

1. What do you remember about the first time you attended this group?

2. How did you feel about opening up in this group and sharing your story?

3. What was the funniest thing that happened in this group?

4. What was the high point for you in this group?

5. What will you miss most about this group?

6. How would you like this group to stay in touch with each other after you multiply?

7. How did this group contribute to your life?

8. What is the biggest change that has occurred in your life since joining this group?

Wild Predictions

Try to match the people in your group to the crazy forecasts below. (Don't take it too seriously; it's meant to be fun!) Read out loud the first item and ask everyone to call out the name of the person who is most likely to accomplish this feat. Then, read the next item and ask everyone to make a new prediction, etc.

THE PERSON IN OUR GROUP MOST LIKELY TO ...

Be the used-car salesperson of the year

Replace Regis Philbin on *Regis and Kathie Lee*

Replace Vanna White on *Wheel of Fortune*

Rollerblade across the country

Open a charm school for Harley-Davidson bikers

Discover a new use for underarm deodorant

Run a dating service for lonely singles

Rise to the top in the CIA

Appear on the cover of *Muscle & Fitness Magazine*

Win the Iditarod dogsled race in Alaska

Make a fortune on pay toilet rentals

Write a best-selling novel based on their love life

Get listed in the *Guinness Book of World Records* for marathon dancing

Win the blue ribbon at the state fair for best Rocky Mountain oyster recipe

Bungee jump off the Golden Gate Bridge

Be the first woman to win the Indianapolis 500

Win the *MAD Magazine* award for worst jokes

Reflection Bible Study

Barnabas and Saul Sent Off — Acts 13:1–3, NIV

13 *In the church at Antioch there were prophets and teachers: Barnabas, Simeon called Niger, Lucius of Cyrene, Manaen (who had been brought up with Herod the tetrarch) and Saul. ²While they were worshiping the Lord and fasting, the Holy Spirit said, "Set apart for me Barnabas and Saul for the work to which I have called them." ³So after they had fasted and prayed, they placed their hands on them and sent them off.*

1. Why do you think God chose this small group in Antioch to launch the first missionary journey (instead of the church headquarters in Jerusalem)?
   - ❏ It was merely coincidental.
   - ❏ They were following the leading of the Holy Spirit.
   - ❏ They were a bunch of outcasts from the fringe of the church.
   - ❏ They didn't know how to "paint inside the lines."

2. How do you think the leadership back in Jerusalem felt when they heard what these guys were doing?
   - ❏ thrilled
   - ❏ embarrassed
   - ❏ angry that they didn't follow protocol
   - ❏ They probably didn't hear about it until later.

3. Why do you think the small group chose two people to send out instead of one?
   - ❏ for companionship
   - ❏ They had different gifts: Paul was a hothead, Barnabas an encourager.
   - ❏ It was coincidental.

4. As you think about sending out some members of your small group to give "birth" to a new group, what is your greatest concern for these people?
   - ❏ keeping the faith
   - ❏ keeping the vision
   - ❏ keeping their personal walk with Christ
   - ❏ keeping in touch with us for support

5. As one who is going to lead or colead a new group, how would you describe your emotions right now?
   - ❏ a nervous wreck
   - ❏ pregnant with excitement
   - ❏ delivery room jitters
   - ❏ Ask me next week.

6. If you could say one word of encouragement to those who are going to be new leaders, what would it be?
   - ❏ I'll be praying for you.
   - ❏ Call me anytime.
   - ❏ You can do it.
   - ❏ It's okay to fail.

What do we do next?
For those who are going to stay with the "mother group," you need to decide on your new covenant and who you are going to invite to fill the empty chairs left by the departing "missionaries."

Do we ever meet again?
Definitely! Plan NOW for "homecoming" next year when the new group returns for a time of celebration. Four good times: the World Series, Super Bowl, Final Four and Stanley Cup.

Group Covenant

Any group can benefit from creating or renewing a group covenant. Take some time for those remaining in the "mother group" to discuss the following questions. When everyone in the group has the same expectations for the group, everything runs more smoothly.

1. The purpose of our group is:

2. The goals of our group are:

3. We will meet for _____ weeks, after which we will decide if we wish to continue as a group. If we do decide to continue, we will reconsider this covenant.

4. We will meet _____ (weekly, every other week, monthly).

5. Our meetings will be from _____ o'clock to _____ o'clock, and we will strive to start and end on time.

6. We will meet at _____
   or rotate from house to house.

7. We will take care of the following details: ❐ child care   ❐ refreshments

8. We agree to the following rules for our group:

   ❐ PRIORITY: While we are in this group, group meetings have priority.

   ❐ PARTICIPATION: Everyone is given the right to their own opinion and all questions are respected.

   ❐ CONFIDENTIALITY: Anything said in the meeting is not to be repeated outside the meeting.

   ❐ EMPTY CHAIR: The group stays open to new people and invites prospective members to visit the group.

   ❐ SUPPORT: Permission is given to call each other in times of need.

   ❐ ADVICE GIVING: Unsolicited advice is not allowed.

   ❐ MISSION: We will do everything in our power to start a new group.

2. What indications of faith do you see in each of these people as they come to Jesus for help?

a.

c.

b.

d.

3. Based on what Jesus was able to do in these four situations, what kind of authority, power or ability did he prove he possessed?

a.

c.

b.

d.

4. Why do you think some people (v. 34) saw the miracles Jesus performed and yet rejected his spiritual leadership?

5. Why do you feel that some people (such as those in these stories) have the faith to ask Jesus to help them, while others never ask for help?

APPLY
1. Spiritually, which character(s) do you identify with most in this passage? Why?
   ❐ The ruler—I was drawn to Jesus only when my situation was desperate; I had nowhere else to go.
   ❐ The woman—I looked for something or someone to restore my brokenness for a long time before I met Jesus.
   ❐ The blind men—In spite of my limitations, somehow I tightly grasped onto Jesus as the one who would restore and save me.
   ❐ The demon-possessed man—I have been freed from the forces that seemed beyond my control.
   ❐ The crowd—I'm not sure what to make of Jesus, but he sure impresses me.
   ❐ The Pharisees—I am very suspicious of all this. I think there are other explanations.

2. If Jesus were passing through your town, would you attempt to talk to him? What need would you ask him to meet in your life?

GROUP AGENDA

After the first part, read the Scripture out loud and divide into groups of 4. Then come back together for the third part.

TO BEGIN / 10–15 Min. (Choose 1 or 2)

1. What is your "family remedy" for a cold?

2. What is the sickest you have ever been?

3. Who do you know who has had a miraculous or amazing physical healing?

TO GO DEEPER / 30 Min. (Choose 2 or 3)

1. If you have completed the homework, choose one of the READ or SEARCH questions and share your answer. (It's okay if more than one person chooses the same question.)

2. The author of this Gospel is Matthew, whom you met in the previous session as Levi. He was a Jew and wrote this Gospel to convince other Jews that Jesus was the Messiah. Why would these miracles be so important to him and his writing?

3. How do you feel about healing today? What is Jesus' role? What is your role?

4. When do you remember being the most desperate for God's help?

5. What current situation in your life seems most desperate or hopeless? What do these stories encourage you to do?

6. CASE STUDY: Jan called on the elders of the church to pray for her healing (as the Scriptures recommend in the book of James), but she died of cancer. Some of the members of your group are struggling with this. What help can you offer for those who had their faith shattered?

TO CLOSE / 15–30 Min.

1. Are you thinking and dreaming about your group's mission? (See the center section.)

2. If your body could say something to you right now, what would it say to you about your lifestyle?

3. How did you answer the questions in APPLY?

4. How can the group help you in prayer?

NOTES

Summary. Opposition or not, Jesus' ministry flourished. While the leaders railed at him for not being religiously orthodox, Jesus simply went about healing people. In the face of his powerful healings, the words of his critics could not prevail in the hearts and minds of the crowds. The four miracles in this passage show Jesus restoring health, life, sight and speech. As with the other miracles in this section of Matthew's Gospel (8:1–9:38), these miracles are not simply meant to impress Matthew's readers with Jesus' power. They are meant to be pointers to Jesus' identity as the Servant of God who has come to establish the new order of God's kingdom (see Isa. 61:1–3). The very nature of his healings provides insights regarding what the kingdom of God will be like when it is fully revealed. It is a realm of restoration and life. In God's kingdom there is freedom from all types of forces that oppress and destroy. It is a realm inaugurated by Jesus the Messiah. The first three stories stress the importance of faith in Jesus as the means of entering into the goodness of God's realm. The final story reveals the crisis of decision which Jesus produces: while some are amazed and proclaim his praises, others slander and insult him as the devil himself.

9:18 *a ruler.* Mark and Luke indicate that this man was the ruler of the local synagogue. In first-century Israel, the temple in Jerusalem was the sole place for sacrifice and was attended by numerous priests and other officials. In contrast, synagogues were found in each city and town where people met weekly on the Sabbath for worship and instruction. Synagogues were run by a committee of lay people (the rulers) who were responsible for the care of the building and for arranging services.

knelt before him. In contrast to the skepticism and criticism of the religious authorities in the passages just prior to this story (see Unit 5), this man comes with reverence and respect for Jesus. In light of the opposition Jesus has received from the official leaders of the people, it could not have been easy for this man, a leader in his community, to humble himself before Jesus in this way. However, his concern for his daughter outweighed his pride.

put your hand on her. The laying on of hands was a common practice used for ordination, for blessing and for healing.

9:20–22 As Jesus travels to the man's home, he is met by a woman with a chronic illness.

9:20 *a woman who had been subject to bleeding.* This woman was probably hemorrhaging from the womb. In addition to the obvious physical weakness such a chronic problem would produce, this particular problem rendered her ritually impure or unclean (see Lev. 15:25–30). As a result, she was not allowed to take part in temple worship, was unable to have any sexual relations with her husband, and was not supposed to be present in a crowd where others might brush up against her and also become "unclean." The long-term effects of this stigma must have eroded her marriage, her self-concept and her relationship with God.

9:21 *touch his cloak.* This woman had heard of Jesus' power and took the chance that he might heal her. Perhaps out of fear of rejection because she was "unclean," she did not even dare approach Jesus openly like the ruler. She simply wanted to touch his cloak without drawing any attention to herself at all. In a quasi-magical way, the power of a person was thought to be transferred to his or her clothing. The ruler thought that his daughter could be healed by Jesus' touch (v. 14). This woman thought she could be healed by touching his clothing.

9:22 *Take heart, daughter.* Jesus not only had power to heal her body; his words are intended to heal her spirit as he affirms her as a true child of God.

your faith has healed you. It was her faith that impelled her to reach out to Jesus—the source of healing power. Jesus' words point out that there is no magic involved in his healing. It is a matter of God's response to her faith in reaching out to him. The word Jesus uses to tell her she is healed comes from the same root as "salvation" and "Savior." Spiritual as well as physical healing is in view here.

9:24 *The girl is not dead but asleep.* Jesus does not mean by this that she has not really died but instead is in some sort of coma. The presence of the mourners ("the flute players and the noisy crowd") and the laughter that greeted this statement all say the same thing: the child was truly dead. Jesus uses this same expression in reference to Lazarus, and he was clearly dead. His body had even begun to decompose (John 11:11–15). What he means is that she is not permanently dead.

9:25 *she got up.* Jesus raises her from the dead.

9:27–34 These next two stories not only continue to emphasize Jesus' miraculous ability to heal; but the giving of sight to the blind and speech to the mute are especially intended to be seen as signs that he is indeed the Messiah who has come to bring sight and speech to his people (Isa. 35:5–6; see also Matt. 11:2–6). Through Jesus, the time of God's redemption of his people has arrived.

9:27 *two blind men.* Blindness was common in the ancient world, often due to infection. Blindness was of various sorts. The most widespread condition was ophthalmia, a form of conjunctivitis that was highly contagious. It was transmitted by flies and was aggravated by the dust and glare of the arid Middle Eastern environment. Blindness also resulted from glaucoma and cataracts, and was sometimes present at birth.

Have mercy on us. Mercy is not as much an emotion as it is concrete aid.

Son of David. This is a clear Messianic title, since there was a strong expectation based upon OT prophecies that the Messiah would be a king in the line of David. The Messiah was understood to have the power to heal (see Matt. 11:4–5). In their cry for mercy, the blind men set the example for how people enter God's kingdom. They understand their need for God's help and believe that in Jesus this help can be found.

9:29 *According to your faith.* As with the story of the woman (v. 14), faith in Christ is shown to be the key that provides access to God's gracious power. The point is that God delights to respond to those who place their hope in him. But God is not a genie, nor is faith the magic lamp that gets God to do what one wants.

9:30 Jesus continues to be concerned that his ministry of healing individuals will obscure his greater task, which is to save people from their sins (Matt. 1:21).

9:32–34 The fourth and final healing in this section is an exorcism which restores speech to a mute. It also functions to summarize the meaning of the miracles in Matthew 8–9. The miracles force people to make choices about Jesus. Either they are seen as signs that draw people to Jesus (v. 33), or are viewed as fraudulent, leading people to take entrenched positions of hostility against him (v. 34).

9:32 The man's affliction is attributed to a demon (see also Matt. 12:22).

9:33 *mute.* This word can mean either deaf or dumb or both.

UNIT 7—Jesus the Messiah / Mark 8:27-38

Peter's Confession of Christ

²⁷Jesus and his disciples went on to the villages around Caesarea Philippi. On the way he asked them, "Who do people say I am?"

²⁸They replied, "Some say John the Baptist; others say Elijah; and still others, one of the prophets."

²⁹"But what about you?" he asked. "Who do you say I am?"

Peter answered, "You are the Christ."

³⁰Jesus warned them not to tell anyone about him.

Jesus Predicts His Death

³¹He then began to teach them that the Son of Man must suffer many things and be rejected by the elders, chief priests and teachers of the law, and that he must be killed and after three days
rise again. *³²He spoke plainly about this, and Peter took him aside and began to rebuke him.*

³³But when Jesus turned and looked at his disciples, he rebuked Peter. "Get behind me, Satan!" he said. "You do not have in mind the things of God, but the things of men."

³⁴Then he called the crowd to him along with his disciples and said: "If anyone would come after me, he must deny himself and take up his cross and follow me. ³⁵For whoever wants to save his life will lose it, but whoever loses his life for me and for the gospel will save it. ³⁶What good is it for a man to gain the whole world, yet forfeit his soul? ³⁷Or what can a man give in exchange for his soul? ³⁸If anyone is ashamed of me and my words in this adulterous and sinful generation, the Son of Man will be ashamed of him when he comes in his Father's glory with the holy angels."

READ

First Reading / First Impressions: Which of the following emotions do you think Peter felt in this passage (check two)?

❏ elation   ❏ shock   ❏ fear   ❏ hope   ❏ shame

❏ anger   ❏ confusion   ❏ peace   ❏ disillusionment   ❏ other:_____

Second Reading / Big Idea: What do you think is the main point Jesus wants his disciples to learn?

SEARCH

1. In asking his disciples, "Who do people say I am?" Jesus seems to be leading up to the crucial question in all of Mark's Gospel (vv. 27–29). What is that question and why is it so important for the disciples?

2. Although Peter correctly identifies Jesus' role, what do verses 31–32 show about the vastly different ideas Peter and Jesus have about "the Christ" (see note on 8:31–38)?

Peter expects the Christ to:

Jesus says the Christ will:

36

3. Why do you think Jesus reacted so strongly to Peter's rebuke (vv. 32–33; see notes)? In what way might Peter's opposition to Jesus' impending death be similar to one of the temptations Jesus faced from Satan (see Unit 2)?

4. Mark's Gospel was probably written to the church in Rome when it was undergoing severe persecution (including crucifixion) at the hands of Emperor Nero. Put yourself in the position of a member of that church. You have seen friends executed because they were Christians. You live with the anxiety that one day you also might be dragged to court and threatened with torture or death unless you deny allegiance to Christ. What lessons are here for you in verses 34–38?

5. What is the significance of Jesus calling the crowd, along with the disciples, to hear these words (v. 34)?

6. From this passage, how would you describe to someone what it means to follow Christ?

APPLY
1. What kinds of behaviors might demonstrate that you are ashamed of Jesus (see v. 38)?

2. What is one area now (in a relationship, a lifestyle choice, an ordering of priorities, the use of resources, the way you work, etc.) where you experience tension between Jesus' way and your way? How does this passage affect the way you intend to deal with that tension?

GROUP AGENDA

After the first part, read the Scripture out loud and divide into groups of 4. Then come back together for the third part.

TO BEGIN / 10–15 Min. (Choose 1 or 2)

1. Have you written a will? Where do you keep it?

2. If you knew that you only had six months to live, what would you do differently?

3. Do you wear a cross? How come?

TO GO DEEPER / 30 Min. (Choose 2 or 3)

1. In the READ and SEARCH sections, what impressed you the most in answering the questions and reading the notes?

2. If you asked the typical person today, "Who is Jesus Christ?" what would they say?

3. What is *your* answer to the question, "Who is Jesus Christ?" How has your answer changed over time?

4. Christianity has been interpreted by some as "Be good to yourself ... you are the captain of your own fate." What would this Scripture passage have to say about this?

5. If professing to be a Christian caused believers to lose their job, family or freedom, what would happen to your church?

6. CASE STUDY: "It doesn't matter what you believe in, as long as you believe in something." This is the way one person in Tom's support group explained what the "second step" meant to him as a recovering alcoholic. Tom chose to make his support group his "higher power." And so far, it seems to be working. Tom wants to join your Bible study group. What do you say?

TO CLOSE / 15–30 Min.

1. Are you happy with your group's progress on developing your mission?

2. Share your answer to one or two of the questions in APPLY.

3. How can the group help you in prayer this week?

NOTES

Summary. This is a pivotal point in the Gospel of Mark. For the first time, after many incidents that demonstrate Jesus' authority over all types of forces, the disciples indicate that they recognize Jesus as the Messiah. However, they still have the wrong idea about the nature and role of the Messiah.

8:28 *Some say.* The people are not clear about just who Jesus is, but tend to see him as one who paves the way for the Messiah. Some (like Herod— Mark 6:16) think he is John the Baptist come back to life. Others think he is the ancient prophet Elijah (1 Kings 17–2 Kings 2), considered to be one of the greatest prophets of Israel who would appear again one day as the forerunner of the Messiah (Mal. 4:5; Mark 9:11–13). Still others are not willing to say which prophet he is, only that he is a prophet who has a message from God.

8:29 *Who do you say I am?* This is the crucial question in Mark's Gospel. With it the author is not only telling the story of the disciples' growth in their faith, but he forces his readers to consider how they will answer the question as well.

Christ. Peter correctly identifies him as the Christ, the Greek term for the Hebrew word Messiah. See note on Luke 2:11 in Unit 1.

8:30 *not to tell anyone.* Jesus urges them to be silent about what they know. While they know he is the Messiah, they do not yet know what kind of Messiah he is. This recognition of who Jesus is follows immediately after the strange two-stage healing of the blind man (Mark 8:22–26). The placement of this story indicates that the healing was meant to be an illustration of the disciples' growing understanding of who Jesus was. Like the blind man, the disciples received the "first touch" of healing. Their spiritual blindness, which, so far, prevented them from understanding Jesus, is beginning to be healed, but they are not yet totally restored to full sight—as the next incident shows (Mark 8:31–33).

8:31–38 Having discovered that Jesus is the Messiah, the disciples now need to know what kind of Messiah he is. He is not, as their culture led them to believe, a nationalistic hero who would lead a literal army in a triumphant battle against Roman oppressors. In the second half of his Gospel, Mark describes the nature of Jesus' messiahship. In this section (Mark 8:31–10:45), the disciples discover he is the Son of Man who came to die for others.

8:31 To predict one's death is rare, but not unknown. To predict that one will then rise from the dead, however, is startling. No wonder the disciples had trouble taking in what Jesus was saying. The fact that this prediction is repeated in Mark's Gospel (9:9,31; 10:33–34) draws attention to its central importance in understanding who Jesus is.

Son of Man. This is the title that Jesus prefers for himself. In the first century it was a rather colorless, indeterminate title (with some messianic overtones) which could be translated as "man" or even "I." This allows Jesus through his teaching to fill it with new meaning and to convey what kind of Messiah he actually is. See also the note on John 1:51 in Unit 4.

rejected by the elders, chief priests and teachers of the law. These three groups made up the Sanhedrin, the ruling Jewish body. While ultimately under Roman supervision, the Sanhedrin had the power to rule in cases involving Jewish law. Jesus is predicting that he will be officially rejected by Israel (see Mark 14:55).

must be killed. The death of the Messiah at the hands of Israel's official governing body played no part in popular ideas about the Messiah. This was a startling, incomprehensible announcement. Jesus knew that his death was mandated by God. It was prophesied in the vision of the Suffering Servant of the Lord in Isaiah 53, and the suffering of the righteous man in Psalm 22.

after three days rise again. This likewise was an unprecedented teaching regarding the Messiah.

8:32 *He spoke plainly.* This is in contrast to his usual style of teaching in parables, the meaning of which was sometimes veiled or obscure. This is exactly what is going to happen.

rebuke. Peter, who moments before identified Jesus as the Messiah, is startled by this teaching. It went so much against his notion of what the Messiah should do. He felt compelled to take Jesus aside and urge him to stop this line of teaching.

8:33 *Get behind me, Satan!* Satan's essential temptation was to persuade Jesus to avoid the way of the cross on his way to receiving the kingdom (Matt. 4:8–10). To do so, however, would require that Jesus abandon his loyalty to the Father. While Peter's objection is motivated by concern, Jesus recognizes it as another appeal for him to turn away from the Father's will. This is not a rejection of Peter's genuine concern, but a dramatic way of expressing Jesus' determination not to allow anything or anyone to dissuade him from following the path God has set for him.

the things of God / the things of men. Peter was concerned with the establishment of a powerful Jewish kingdom ruled by Jesus. Jesus was concerned with the Father's will for a universal kingdom in which all people who believed in him would be reconciled to God and one another through the sacrificial death of Jesus for their sins.

8:34–38 Jesus defines what following him means. It is not glory and magic. It involves denial, cross-bearing and losing one's life.

8:34 *he called the crowd ... along with his disciples.* By this phrase, Mark is showing that this message is intended to be heard by *everyone* who wishes to follow Jesus.

come after me. Discipleship is a matter of following the ways of one's teacher.

deny himself / take up his cross / follow me. To "take up a cross" was something done by a person sentenced to death by crucifixion. This would fill the minds of Mark's readers with memories of their comrades who had been executed in this way by Nero (under the charge that to be a Christian was an act of treason to Rome). This stark image points out the fact that to be a follower of Jesus means that loyalty to him precedes all desires and ambitions, including the natural desire for self-preservation. Like Jesus, his followers are to single-mindedly pursue God's way, even when it means suffering and death.

8:35 *save his life.* The image is of a trial in which one is called upon to renounce Jesus in order to live. This would have immediate application to the Christians in Rome, who were pressed with the decision of considering whether to affirm their loyalty to Jesus (and face the persecution of the state) or deny their association with Jesus (and be allowed to live).

will lose it. That is, the person will ultimately face the judgment of God for his or her denial of Christ.

whoever loses his life ... will save it. The person who steadfastly maintains loyalty to Jesus, even in the face of death, has the sure hope of the eternal life to come.

8:38 *ashamed of me.* This would be revealed by failing to persist in one's Christian testimony in times of persecution.

UNIT 8—The Transfiguration / Mark 9:2-13

The Transfiguration

²After six days Jesus took Peter, James and John with him and led them up a high mountain, where they were all alone. There he was transfigured before them. ³His clothes became dazzling white, whiter than anyone in the world could bleach them. ⁴And there appeared before them Elijah and Moses, who were talking with Jesus.

⁵Peter said to Jesus, "Rabbi, it is good for us to be here. Let us put up three shelters—one for you, one for Moses and one for Elijah." ⁶(He did not know what to say, they were so frightened.)

⁷Then a cloud appeared and enveloped them, and a voice came from the cloud: "This is my Son, whom I love. Listen to him!"

⁸Suddenly, when they looked around, they no longer saw anyone with them except Jesus.

⁹As they were coming down the mountain, Jesus gave them orders not to tell anyone what they had seen until the Son of Man had risen from the dead. ¹⁰They kept the matter to themselves, discussing what "rising from the dead" meant.

¹¹And they asked him, "Why do the teachers of the law say that Elijah must come first?"

¹²Jesus replied, "To be sure, Elijah does come first, and restores all things. Why then is it written that the Son of Man must suffer much and be rejected? ¹³But I tell you, Elijah has come, and they have done to him everything they wished, just as it is written about him."

READ

First Reading / First Impressions: What stands out the most to you from this story?
- ❏ Jesus' transformation
- ❏ Peter's reaction
- ❏ God's speaking

Second Reading / Big Idea: Like the passage in the last unit, this is a passage loaded with emotions. What words would you use to describe the emotional state of the disciples in this story (check two)?

- ❏ elation
- ❏ shock
- ❏ fear
- ❏ hope
- ❏ shame
- ❏ anger
- ❏ confusion
- ❏ peace
- ❏ disillusionment
- ❏ other:_____

SEARCH

1. As the baptism of Jesus (see Unit 2) opened the first section of Mark's Gospel, so the Transfiguration opens the second. What parallels do you see between these two events (see "Summary" in notes)?

2. The mountain, the dazzling light, Elijah, Moses, the cloud and the voice are all reminders of special times in the past when God revealed himself (see notes). What does this scene say about Jesus?

3. Why do you think Jesus took these three disciples with him—even though he didn't want them to tell anyone what happened (v. 9)?

4. Malachi 4:5–6 prophesies that Elijah would return prior to the coming of the Messiah. In what way does Jesus indicate this prophecy is fulfilled (see note on v. 12)?

5. How could Elijah's and John the Baptist's experience help the disciples understand the nature of Jesus' messiahship (see note on v. 13)?

APPLY
1. What is your Mount of Transfiguration—that is, a time or place where you glimpsed a bit of Jesus' glory in a special way (e.g., a special worship service, church retreat, during a crisis, etc.)?

2. Like the disciples, many Christians have an idea that following the Messiah ought to insulate them from all harm. How does Jesus' sobering picture of a glorious yet suffering Messiah shape your view of what the Christian life is really all about?

GROUP AGENDA

After the first part, read the Scripture out loud and divide into groups of 4. Then come back together for the third part.

TO BEGIN / 10–15 Min. (Choose 1 or 2)
1. What's the highest place you have ever climbed?

2. If you could choose three friends to go with you on a spiritual retreat, who would you choose and where would you go?

3. How good are you at keeping secrets?

TO GO DEEPER / 30 Min. (Choose 2 or 3)
1. If you have completed the homework, what stands out to you from READ or SEARCH?

2. If you had been Peter (without the benefit of hindsight), how would you have reacted to all of this?

3. In what way could this experience only make sense after Jesus was raised from the dead?

4. The disciples were told (v. 7), "This is my Son, whom I love. Listen to him!" What is the most effective way for you to listen to God? What keeps you from being a better listener?

5. CASE STUDY: John was laid off from work six months ago and the bank is threatening to foreclose on their mortgage. He asks you why God is allowing him and his family to suffer like this. From this passage and from your own experience, what can you say?

TO CLOSE / 15–30 Min.
1. Has your group assigned three people as a leadership core to start a new small group?

2. How did you answer the questions in APPLY?

3. How would you describe your relationship with God right now: In the valley? Climbing the mountain? On the mountaintop? On the rocks?

4. How can the group pray for you?

NOTES

Summary. Events begin to gather speed. The disciples have discovered that Jesus is no mere teacher (no matter how gifted and special he is), nor is he simply a prophet (no matter how powerful he might be). He is the Messiah—God's anointed servant who has come to bring a new order in the world. The remaining units focus on how Jesus opens the way into the kingdom of God by his death and resurrection. Here in the Transfiguration, God affirms once again that Jesus is his beloved Son, and he declares to the people (via the three apostles who witness these events) that Jesus is, indeed, the promised one whose coming was foretold in the OT. The account of the Transfiguration is similar to the baptism of Jesus (Mark 1:9–11) in some interesting ways. The baptism of Jesus opened the first half of the Gospel of Mark (after some preliminary words from the OT and from John the Baptist). The Transfiguration opens the second half following some defining words by Jesus. In both incidents, the voice of God affirms that Jesus is his special Son. Both draw heavily on the OT for their meaning. As the baptism of Jesus foreshadows his death, so the Transfiguration foreshadows his resurrection.

9:2 *After six days.* With this phrase Mark connects the Transfiguration with Jesus' prediction that "some who are standing here will not taste death before they see the kingdom of God come with power" (Mark 9:1).

Peter, James and John. These three apostles come to form a sort of inner circle around Jesus. Mark has already pointed out that Jesus took only these three disciples with him when he raised Jairus' daughter (Mark 5:37–43).

a high mountain. This may well be Mt. Hermon, a mountain 9,000 feet high located 12 miles from Caesarea Philippi (though early tradition says it is Mt. Tabor located southwest of the Sea of Galilee). The physical location of the mountain is not as significant as its theological meaning. Mountains were the places where God revealed himself to the leaders of Israel in special ways. For example, God appeared to Moses on Mt. Sinai (Ex. 24) and to the prophet Elijah on Mt. Horeb (1 Kings 19).

transfigured. The word used here is *metamorphothe* (from which the English word "metamorphosis" comes). It literally means "to change one's form."

9:3 *dazzling white.* Here the disciples witness Jesus as he is changed into a form just like God. In Revelation 1:9–18, the resurrected, glorified Jesus is described in similar terms. Brilliant, radiant light is often associated with appearances of God in the OT (see Dan. 7:9).

9:4 *Elijah.* Elijah was a great prophet. Rather than dying, he was taken up to heaven by God (2 Kings 2:1–12). The Jews expected that he would return just prior to the coming of the salvation they had been promised (Mal. 4:5–6). His presence on the mountain is to indicate that, indeed, he has come to bear witness to Jesus as the Messiah.

Moses. Moses was the greatest figure in Israel's history and tradition. He was the one to whom God gave the Law, which became the very heart of the nation. And it was Moses who prophesied that God would one day send another prophet to lead his people: "The LORD your God will raise up for you a prophet like me from among your own brothers. You must listen to him" (Deut. 18:15). The early Christians took this to be a prophecy about Jesus (Acts 3:22–26; 7:35–37). The presence of both Moses and Elijah on the mountain is meant to indicate that the OT Law and the Prophets, which form the core of Israel's identity, endorse Jesus as God's appointed Messiah. They witness to his greatness and superiority over them.

9:5 *shelters.* Peter might have had in mind the huts of intertwined branches that were put up at the Festival of Tabernacles to commemorate Israel's time in the wilderness. Or he might be thinking of the "tent of meeting" where God met with Moses. In making this suggestion, Peter shows his quite understandable confusion about this event. Did it mark the full arrival of the kingdom? Did this mean that Jesus had come into his glory without the suffering he told them about?

9:6 *frightened.* Throughout the Bible, whenever God is manifested before people, the human response is one of fear and being undone.

9:7 *a cloud.* The OT often speaks of clouds as one of the phenomena which accompanies an appearance of God. Clouds are signs of his majesty and serve to veil his full glory from the eyes of mortals (who would otherwise be totally overwhelmed).

a voice. Once again, as at the baptism of Jesus (Mark 1:11), God declares that Jesus is his Son.

This is my Son, whom I love. By means of this incident, it is revealed that not only is Jesus the Messiah (as the disciples have just confessed), he

is also the Son of God. Both titles are necessary for a full understanding of his nature and role.

Listen to him! This is a quotation from Moses' great prophecy about the coming prophet (Deut. 18:15). The new prophet, whose authority and glory would supersede that of Moses, was on the scene. This is a divine testimony to his authority.

9:8 In an instant, the overwhelming experience of God's glory was gone. Moses, Elijah and God himself had all borne witness to these three disciples regarding the person of Jesus. Mark has answered once and for all the question about Jesus' identity which had been building throughout the first eight chapters of his Gospel.

9:9–11 What must have seemed so clear on the mountain became obscure as the disciples walked down. Jesus again introduces the thought of his impending death, which to the disciples seems totally out of context with what they have just experienced. They wonder if there is some other meaning to the notion of "rising from the dead." Then their thoughts run to the meaning of the Jewish expectation that Elijah will come to inaugurate the kingdom. Was that what had happened on the mountain?

9:9 *not to tell.* The meaning of this event cannot be understood until Jesus dies and rises again. Then it will be clear what kind of Messiah he is and what it means to be the Son of God.

9:12 *To be sure, Elijah does come first.* Here in the Transfiguration the long-expected Elijah comes. However, as verse 13 shows, Jesus asserts that Elijah has come in a second sense. John the Baptist came in the spirit and power of Elijah by being the forerunner of the Messiah.

9:13 While it seems incongruous to the disciples that the Messiah must suffer, Jesus reminds them that Elijah himself suffered at the hands of King Ahab and Queen Jezebel (1 Kings 19:1–10). John the Baptist suffered and died at the hands of Herod and Herodias (see Mark 6:14–29), paralleling Elijah's experience in the past. John's suffering and death foreshadow what awaits Jesus as well. Jesus is shattering the illusion that God's anointed messengers move easily into triumph. Elijah and John are two great men of God from Israel's past and present who were rejected and persecuted by the leaders of the people. Thus, it should come as no surprise to learn that the Messiah himself will experience the same rejection.

UNIT 9—The Lord's Supper / Mark 14:12-26

The Lord's Supper

¹²On the first day of the Feast of Unleavened Bread, when it was customary to sacrifice the Passover lamb, Jesus' disciples asked him, "Where do you want us to go and make preparations for you to eat the Passover?"

¹³So he sent two of his disciples, telling them, "Go into the city, and a man carrying a jar of water will meet you. Follow him. ¹⁴Say to the owner of the house he enters, 'The Teacher asks: Where is my guest room, where I may eat the Passover with my disciples?' ¹⁵He will show you a large upper room, furnished and ready. Make preparations for us there."

¹⁶The disciples left, went into the city and found things just as Jesus had told them. So they prepared the Passover.

¹⁷When evening came, Jesus arrived with the Twelve. ¹⁸While they were reclining at the table eating, he said, "I tell you the truth, one of you will betray me—one who is eating with me."

¹⁹They were saddened, and one by one they said to him, "Surely not I?"

²⁰"It is one of the Twelve," he replied, "one who dips bread into the bowl with me. ²¹The Son of Man will go just as it is written about him. But woe to that man who betrays the Son of Man! It would be better for him if he had not been born."

²²While they were eating, Jesus took bread, gave thanks and broke it, and gave it to his disciples, saying, "Take it; this is my body."

²³Then he took the cup, gave thanks and offered it to them, and they all drank from it.

²⁴"This is my blood of the covenant, which is poured out for many," he said to them. ²⁵"I tell you the truth, I will not drink again of the fruit of the vine until that day when I drink it anew in the kingdom of God."

²⁶When they had sung a hymn, they went out to the Mount of Olives.

READ

First Reading / First Impressions: The Passover Feast was supposed to be a time of great anticipation. How would you describe the mood in this passage?

❏ somber, foreboding　　　❏ anxious, tense　　　❏ bleak, depressing　　　❏ relaxed, pleasant

Second Reading / Big Idea: Just from your initial impression, what do you think was going through Jesus' mind at this time?

SEARCH

1. Why were the secret arrangements necessary for this Passover meal (see note on 14:13–16)?

2. How do these key Passover elements from Exodus 12 parallel the events which are happening in the life of Jesus?

lamb without blemish chosen:

lamb sacrificed:

blood on the door frame:

3. Is verse 21 a warning only to Judas, the betrayer, or to others who turn their backs on Jesus? (Remember, Mark was writing to Christians facing persecution.)

4. Jesus leads the disciples in the first Lord's Supper by taking some of the Passover elements and giving them new meaning. How does Jesus reinterpret these two elements (see notes)?

	Passover Meaning	Jesus' New Interpretation
Bread:		
Cup:		

5. What is different about the circumstances of the first Lord's Supper and the celebration of it in the church today?

6. Why is the Lord's Supper important to believers?

APPLY

1. How would you explain the meaning and the purpose of the Lord's Supper to someone who witnessed this celebration at your church for the first time?

2. If we are not careful, rituals like the Lord's Supper can lose their significance and become mundane or impersonal. What could you (and the group) do before the next Lord's Supper to increase the significance of this celebration for you (e.g., reflect on the Last Supper account in the Bible, spend time in prayer, etc.)?

GROUP AGENDA

After the first part, read the Scripture out loud and divide into groups of 4. Then come back together for the third part.

TO BEGIN / 10–15 Min. (Choose 1 or 2)

1. As a child, what were mealtimes like? Who sat where around the table?

2. What are the special meals in your family now: Thanksgiving? Christmas? Sunday dinner? Birthday suppers?

3. Who is the storyteller in your family? Are there any special reminders of your family heritage that you cherish?

TO GO DEEPER / 30 Min. (Choose 2 or 3)

1. Choose one of the questions in READ or SEARCH and share your answer.

2. From the notes, what did you learn about the meaning behind the Lord's Supper that you did not know before (or what were you reminded of that was significant to you)?

3. Do you think that the disciples understood what Jesus was saying when he said, "This is my blood"? How many people in your church really understand what the Lord's Supper is all about?

4. When did you come to understand the real meaning of the Lord's Supper?

5. If you were at the meal and could have stopped the betrayer, would you? What if you knew what you know now about the Messiah—the Passover Lamb?

6. CASE STUDY: Bill, an Army reserve officer, said, "The Lord's Supper had a lot of meaning for me during the Persian Gulf War when I shared 'the table' with those who really cared about each other. But it doesn't have the same meaning for me now." What made the Lord's Supper so special during the war?

TO CLOSE / 15–30 Min.

1. How did you answer the questions in APPLY?

2. Through both Passover and Christ's death, God brought freedom. What do you need to be free from?

3. How can the group support you in prayer?

NOTES

Summary. The Last Supper plays an important role in Matthew, Mark and Luke. Through this meal, Jesus formally introduces the fact that his death is the means by which a new covenant would be established between God and his people. It is this meal that declares Jesus' continuing presence with his people, and gives meaning to Jesus' death as a sacrifice for sins. At Passover, a lamb was sacrificed as a means of atoning for the sins of the people. In the same way, Jesus' death is a sacrifice which leads God to "pass over" (or forgive) the sins of those who entrust themselves to him.

14:12 *On the first day of the Feast of Unleavened Bread.* The Feast of Unleavened Bread, which commemorated the deliverance of Israel from Egypt (Ex. 12:14–20), did not officially start until the day after the Passover. However, by the first century this feast was coupled with the Passover so that there was a week of feasting. The day on which the lambs were sacrificed was sometimes referred to as the first day of the Feast of Unleavened Bread.

sacrifice the Passover lamb. Passover was a feast in which the people of Israel celebrated how God "passed over" them as he brought judgment upon the Egyptians who had for so long mistreated Israel (see Ex. 12). Each pilgrim sacrificed his own lamb in the temple. A priest caught the blood in a bowl and this was thrown on the altar. After removing parts of the lamb for sacrifice, the carcass was returned to the pilgrim to be roasted and eaten for Passover. Josephus estimated that 250,000 lambs were killed at Passover. On this particular Passover, God would once again rescue his people, though in a totally unexpected way—namely through the death of the Messiah.

make preparations. The disciples would have to set out the unleavened bread and the wine, collect the bitter herbs such as horseradish and chicory (which represented the bitterness of slavery), make the sauce of dried fruit, spices and wine in which the bread was dipped (which represented how the Israelites had to make bricks), and roast the lamb on an open fire (which reminded the people of the lambs which were sacrificed at the original Passover).

eat the Passover. The meal begins with a blessing, the passing of bread, and drinking from the first of four cups of wine. Then psalms are sung and the story of the deliverance read, followed by the second cup of wine and the eating of the bread, herbs and the sauce (into which Judas and the others dip the bread—see v. 20). Then the meal itself, with the roast lamb and the remainder of the bread, is eaten. More prayers are said and the third cup is drunk. More psalms are sung before the final cup is drunk. After that, another psalm is sung. Two short prayers end the feast. The four cups of wine represented the four promises God gave the Israelites in Exodus 6:6–7: (1) "I will bring you out from under the yoke of the Egyptians," (2) "I will free you ..." (3) "I will redeem you ..." and (4) "I will take you as my own people."

14:13–16 Instructions for Jesus' arrest had already been issued (see John 11:57). Since he knew that the officials were looking for him in places away from the crowd, he would generally sleep in Bethany, which was outside the jurisdiction of the priests. However, Jews were required to eat the Passover meal in Jerusalem itself. Hence the need for secret arrangements. The irony is that Jesus knows full well that he will be betrayed from within his own circle of disciples (see Mark 14:18–21; 27–31). Jesus' instructions here parallel those he gave concerning the donkey on which he first rode into the city (see Mark 11:1–6). It seems clear that he has been to Jerusalem previously when he made these arrangements. It is also clear that he is arranging the events so that they happen in such a way as to reveal who he is.

14:13 *a man carrying a jar of water.* Such a person would have been easy to spot and follow since it was highly unusual for a man to carry a jar.

14:17 *When evening came.* The Passover meal could be eaten only after sunset. What followed was a night of eager watching in which people asked: "Will this be the night when God comes again to deliver his people from bondage?"

14:18 *reclining at the table.* People would eat festive meals by lying on couches or cushions arranged around a low table.

I tell you the truth. Literally, this is "Amen," a word used to announce a solemn declaration.

14:20 *one who dips bread into the bowl with me.* This was the bowl of sauce. To eat together was a sign of friendship.

14:21 *The Son of Man will go just as it is written about him.* Passages such as Isaiah 53:1–6 point to the suffering of God's chosen servant.

It would be better for him if he had not been born. This is a stern warning of the judgment to come upon Judas (and others) who turn their backs on Jesus.

14:22–26 Jesus' celebration of the Last Supper provides the model for the way the church came to celebrate Communion (see 1 Cor. 11:23–26). His use of the bread and the cup in a symbolic way (as a means of teaching) was consistent with the way in which the various elements of the Passover meal were used symbolically (e.g., the bowl of salt water was used to remind them of the tears shed in Egypt and of the Red Sea through which they passed). The symbols in the Passover meal pointed back to the first covenant God made with Israel, while Jesus' words here at the Last Supper pointed forward to his death and the new covenant which would result from it.

14:22 *took bread, gave thanks and broke it, and gave it to his disciples.* Commonly at Passover, bread was broken and distributed prior to the meal as a reminder of how God had provided bread for his people in the wilderness. Jesus' action at this point in the meal would be unusual, calling attention to its new, special meaning.

this is my body. Jesus adds a radically new interpretation to the bread. From now on, they are to see it as representing his body. As they share in the bread, they share in his life, mission and destiny.

14:23 *cup.* Lane argues that this was the third cup passed around at the end of the meal. It stood for the promise of redemption. Jesus relates the Passover cup of red wine to the renewal of the covenant of God with his people through his sacrificial death. It is in this way that redemption will truly come.

gave thanks. The Greek word "to give thanks" is *eucharisto,* from which the word Eucharist is derived.

14:24 *covenant.* In general terms, a covenant is a treaty between two parties. Such an agreement was often sealed by the sacrifice of an animal. It refers to the arrangement that God made with Israel (see Ex. 24:1–8) which was dependent on Israel's obedience. Now (as anticipated in Jer. 31:31–33) a new covenant is established which is made dependent on Jesus' obedience (his sacrificial death). A covenant of law becomes a covenant of love.

14:25 *I will not drink again of the fruit of the vine.* Apparently, Jesus does not drink the fourth and final cup, which symbolizes how God has gathered his people to himself. Instead, he will wait until the messianic banquet at the close of the age to celebrate the fulfillment of that promise.

UNIT 10—Gethsemane / Mark 14:32-42

Gethsemane

³²They went to a place called Gethsemane, and Jesus said to his disciples, "Sit here while I pray." ³³He took Peter, James and John along with him, and he began to be deeply distressed and troubled. ³⁴"My soul is overwhelmed with sorrow to the point of death," he said to them. "Stay here and keep watch."

³⁵Going a little farther, he fell to the ground and prayed that if possible the hour might pass from him. ³⁶"Abba,ª Father," he said, "everything is possible for you. Take this cup from me. Yet not what I will, but what you will."

³⁷Then he returned to his disciples and found them sleeping. "Simon," he said to Peter, "are you asleep? Could you not keep watch for one hour? ³⁸Watch and pray so that you will not fall into temptation. The spirit is willing, but the body is weak."

³⁹Once more he went away and prayed the same thing. ⁴⁰When he came back, he again found them sleeping, because their eyes were heavy. They did not know what to say to him.

⁴¹Returning the third time, he said to them, "Are you still sleeping and resting? Enough! The hour has come. Look, the Son of Man is betrayed into the hands of sinners. ⁴²Rise! Let us go! Here comes my betrayer!"

ª36 Aramaic for *Father*

READ
First Reading / First Impressions: From this scene, what image, action or sound makes the greatest impression on you?

Second Reading / Big Idea: What do you think was the hardest part of this experience for Jesus?
- ❏ submitting to God's will
- ❏ being let down by his friends
- ❏ preparing for the cross

SEARCH
1. Why do you think Jesus asked Peter, James and John to accompany him and share in his time of prayer (see note on v. 34)?

2. Looking at verses 33–34, how would you describe Jesus' emotional state? What caused this?

3. People often pray "not my will, but your will be done" when they are unsure about what God's will really is. That is not the case here. God's will is very clear to Jesus. Given that, what does this statement mean to Jesus (see note for v. 36)?

48

4. After denying Jesus shortly after this, how do you think Peter felt about Jesus' warning in verse 38?

5. Why was it important for Jesus to pray? Why was it important for the disciples to pray?

APPLY

1. Why is it important for you to pray?

2. "Yet not what I will, but what you will." How does Jesus' prayer to the Father apply to the concerns in your life today? List the specific areas where you struggle to do God's will.

3. Do you need help in knowing God's will in this matter? If so, who besides God can you call on? Or do you (like Jesus) know God's will, but are struggling with resolving to do it?

4. When it comes to doing the will of God, how would you finish this sentence? "I desire to do God's will ..."
   - ❒ all of the time
   - ❒ most of the time
   - ❒ some of the time
   - ❒ rarely

GROUP AGENDA

After the first part, read the Scripture out loud and divide into groups of 4. Then come back together for the third part.

TO BEGIN / 10–15 Min. (Choose 1 or 2)
1. When have you fallen asleep at an embarrassing moment: In church? In school? At work? During a concert or recital?

2. When you're facing difficult situations, do you want people to be with you or do you prefer being alone?

3. In the past three years, what issue / struggle has caused you the most anguish?

TO GO DEEPER / 30 Min. (Choose 2 or 3)
1. If you have completed the homework, what stands out the most to you in READ or SEARCH?

2. What do you learn about the nature and character of Jesus from this passage and the study notes?

3. Some movies (like *Jesus Christ: Superstar*) have portrayed Jesus in Gethsemane as being confused about his identity and purpose. What do they fail to realize?

4. If Jesus had backed out on his mission, what would have been the consequences?

5. What is the closest you have come to facing your own personal Gethsemane—where you went through a time of soul-searching, anxiety or loneliness?

6. CASE STUDY: Sarah went on a summer mission trip to Bangladesh and saw for the first time what widespread suffering was like. She has since decided to give up her lucrative medical practice and become a medical missionary. Her friends think she is crazy. They ask you to speak to her. What are you going to say?

TO CLOSE / 15–30 Min.
1. How are you doing on your group mission?

2. What did you learn about yourself in APPLY? (Share as much as you feel comfortable.)

3. How does it make you feel to realize that Jesus knows *your* weaknesses and failures, just as he knew Peter's?

4. How can the group help you in prayer?

NOTES

Summary. This scene follows immediately after the Lord's Supper (Unit 9). Two themes dominate this section: Jesus' continued obedience to God (despite his dread of what was coming) and the disciples' continued failure to grasp what lay ahead for Jesus.

14:32 *Gethsemane.* This was an olive orchard in an estate at the foot of the Mount of Olives just outside the eastern wall of Jerusalem. The name literally means "an oil press" (for making olive oil).

14:33 *Peter, James and John.* As in the past, these three men (who form the inner circle around Jesus) accompany Jesus during a time of great significance (see Mark 9:2–8—Unit 8). Interestingly, neither the rebuke of Peter (Mark 8:32), nor the self-centered request of James and John (Mark 10:35–40), nor the warning of Peter's upcoming denial (Mark 14:27–31) has damaged their relationship with Jesus.

deeply distressed. Literally, this is filled with "shuddering awe." Jesus is filled with a deep, deep sorrow as the full impact of what his submission to God will mean overwhelms him.

14:34 *keep watch.* This was an invitation for the disciples to join him in preparation for the severe trial that was soon to come. While it expresses Jesus' desire for human companionship in his time of crisis, it also points out that these men need to prepare themselves as well. Verses 37–41 show that his concern was for how they would face the fact of his arrest and death.

14:35 *a little farther.* A few yards more.

fell to the ground. This accents the emotional distress he was feeling. He is physically overwhelmed by the depth of sorrow and anxiety he feels.

prayed. It was customary at the time for people to pray aloud. Therefore, the disciples heard (and remembered) his prayer. This is the third time in Mark that Jesus has been shown in prayer (see also Mark 1:35; 6:46).

the hour. This word is often used to refer to an event that represents a crucial turning point in God's plan for a person or for the world (see v. 41; also Mark 13:32). In reference to Jesus, it specifically refers to his crucifixion (see also John 12:23ff). Jesus' plea is that there might be some way for God's plan to be fulfilled without him having to face this particular "hour."

14:36 *Abba.* This is Aramaic for "Father." This is how a child would address their father, i.e., "Daddy." This was not a title that was used in prayer in the first century.

this cup. Like the word "hour," "cup" was also used as an image referring to the destiny God had in store for a person. In some cases it refers to "the cup of salvation" the Lord gives his people to drink (Ps. 16:5; 116:13). However, quite often the "cup of the Lord" was used in reference to divine judgment (Ps. 75:8; Isa. 51:17; Jer. 25:15; Ezek. 23:32–33; Rev. 16:19). To experience God's judgment is like being forced to drink large gulps of strong, bitter wine; it leaves a person sick, staggering and totally unable to function. By this image, Jesus acknowledges that his impending death is not simply a human tragedy, but an act of divine judgment (see also Mark 10:38–39). It is this aspect of what he faces that so frightens him. He must drink of the cup of God's wrath against sin.

Yet not what I will, but what you will. This is the classic expression of Jesus' submission to God. While his personal desire was to avoid the cross, his deeper commitment was to do the Father's will even though it included the cross. Today many people tend to use this phrase when they are unsure of what God's will is in their personal situation (i.e., "I pray you will heal my uncle, Lord; but your will, not mine, be done"). This is not the case here. Jesus had no doubt as to what the Father's will was. God's will was horribly clear to him and he recoiled from it. For Jesus, this phrase is an expression of his final resolve. Although the prospect of the cross seemed crushing to him, this statement expresses his commitment to pursue God's will despite the cost.

14:37 *sleeping.* It was very late (the Passover could extend up to midnight) and they had drunk at least four cups of wine in connection with the Passover meal (see notes on Mark 14:12 in Unit 9).

Simon ... are you asleep? Jesus had earlier warned Peter that he would soon disavow ever having known Jesus, a charge Peter denied emphatically (Mark 14:29–31). Despite this warning, even Peter fails to prepare himself for what was to come.

one hour. This time the word is used literally (see note on v. 35). Despite Jesus' clear warning that a major crisis was coming, Peter and the other two disciples could not even keep a relatively short amount of time to prepare themselves.

14:38 *Watch and pray.* To "watch" means to be spiritually alert, lest they fall into the temptation to be unfaithful to God.

temptation. The trial or test that is about to come upon them is not merely something that might cause physical pain. It is one that could lead them to deny their loyalty to God himself.

The spirit is willing, but the body is weak. This is not saying that the disciples' hearts are in the right place, but they are just too tired to do what Jesus says! It is better to translate "body" as "flesh" in that it refers not simply to a person's body but one's human nature.

14:39–40 A second time Jesus goes off to pray, but returns to find the disciples asleep.

14:40 *They did not know what to say to him.* This is reflective of the householder's servants who are left without excuse when confronted with the fact that they have failed to carry out their duties faithfully (Mark 13:36). The disciples simply cannot grasp the pressing importance of the situation they face.

14:41 *the third time.* Jesus had earlier warned Peter that he would deny him three times (Mark 14:30). Now Jesus comes to Peter three times to urge him to pray and become prepared for what is to come. However, as in the other two times, Peter and the others are asleep again.

Are you still sleeping and resting? This is an ironic note of rebuke. Right up to the moment of crisis, the disciples fail to recognize what is happening. They have not prepared themselves at all.

into the hands of sinners. This refers to the religious authorities that Jesus confronted throughout Mark 11:1–13:37 who have corrupted the offices they hold. The irony of this assessment is that the term "sinners" was used by these religious leaders to refer to those Jews who did not live by the Law and to all Gentiles. In fact, it is a term they have earned by their actions.

14:42 *Rise! Let us go!* Having resolved to do the Father's will, Jesus takes the initiative to approach the crowd coming to arrest him. This action illustrates the words of John's Gospel when Jesus declared, "No one takes (my life) from me, but I lay it down of my own accord" (John 10:18).

UNIT 11—Jesus Before Pilate / Mark 15:1-20

Jesus Before Pilate

15 Very early in the morning, the chief priests, with the elders, the teachers of the law and the whole Sanhedrin, reached a decision. They bound Jesus, led him away and handed him over to Pilate.

²"Are you the king of the Jews?" asked Pilate.

"Yes, it is as you say," Jesus replied.

³The chief priests accused him of many things. ⁴So again Pilate asked him, "Aren't you going to answer? See how many things they are accusing you of."

⁵But Jesus still made no reply, and Pilate was amazed.

⁶Now it was the custom at the Feast to release a prisoner whom the people requested. ⁷A man called Barabbas was in prison with the insurrectionists who had committed murder in the uprising. ⁸The crowd came up and asked Pilate to do for them what he usually did.

⁹"Do you want me to release to you the king of the Jews?" asked Pilate, ¹⁰knowing it was out of envy that the chief priests had handed Jesus over to him. ¹¹But the chief priests stirred up the crowd to have Pilate release Barabbas instead.

¹²"What shall I do, then, with the one you call the king of the Jews?" Pilate asked them.

¹³"Crucify him!" they shouted.

¹⁴"Why? What crime has he committed?" asked Pilate.

But they shouted all the louder, "Crucify him!"

¹⁵Wanting to satisfy the crowd, Pilate released Barabbas to them. He had Jesus flogged, and handed him over to be crucified.

The Soldiers Mock Jesus

¹⁶The soldiers led Jesus away into the palace (that is, the Praetorium) and called together the whole company of soldiers. ¹⁷They put a purple robe on him, then twisted together a crown of thorns and set it on him. ¹⁸And they began to call out to him, "Hail, king of the Jews!" ¹⁹Again and again they struck him on the head with a staff and spit on him. Falling on their knees, they paid homage to him. ²⁰And when they had mocked him, they took off the purple robe and put his own clothes on him. Then they led him out to crucify him.

READ

First Reading / First Impressions: If you were a film director, how would you portray Pilate?

❐ as a slick politician

❐ as a wimp

❐ as a victim of circumstances

❐ as a pragmatist—going with the flow

Second Reading / Big Idea: What do you find most amazing about this story?

❐ that Jesus was so silent

❐ that a murderer was released instead of the Messiah

❐ that Jesus allowed all this to happen

❐ that the people turned on Jesus

❐ that Jesus was so misunderstood

❐ that Jesus was so mistreated

SEARCH

1. In an all-night session, the Sanhedrin finds Jesus guilty of blasphemy, a crime deserving death (Mark 14:64). Why did the Jewish authorities have to bring Jesus before Pilate (see "Summary" in notes)?

2. Where were the disciples during this time (see Mark 14:50,72)? Why are they not with Jesus?

3. Why do you think the Sanhedrin, in front of Pilate, accused Jesus of claiming to be the king of the Jews, when in their own trial the charge was blasphemy (see notes)?

4. Why didn't Jesus answer the charges against him (see note on vv. 4–5)?

5. Pilate saw through the chief priests' accusations to their real motivations (v. 10). What did Pilate do based on that insight?

6. Why did Pilate order Jesus flogged and crucified (v. 15)?

7. Why do you think people, like the soldiers (vv. 16–20), wanted to insult, hurt and mock Jesus?

APPLY

1. Sometimes it is not socially acceptable or politically expedient to stand publicly with Jesus. What do you do at those times?

2. Barabbas is an important character in this story. In comparison to his life, which expression best describes your current situation before God?
   - ❒ I am bound in chains, locked in a dungeon, and just waiting for judgment. There is no hope.
   - ❒ I know people are rooting for me, but there's no way I can get out of the mess I've made.
   - ❒ I have found myself set free, but I can't figure out what happened.
   - ❒ I recognize I am free from sin's penalty, because Jesus took my place.
   - ❒ other:_____

3. Sin is part of all our lives. Looking over your life and into your heart, with which characters (the Sanhedrin, Pilate, the crowd, Barabbas, the soldiers, the disciples) can you identify most? Why?

GROUP AGENDA

After the first part, read the Scripture out loud and divide into groups of 4. Then come back together for the third part.

TO BEGIN / 10–15 Min. (Choose 1 or 2)

1. When was the last time you got a traffic ticket? Were you treated fairly by the authorities?

2. How interested do you get in high profile court cases?

3. When someone accuses you of something you didn't do, how do you react?

TO GO DEEPER / 30 Min. (Choose 2 or 3)

1. Choose one of the READ or SEARCH questions to answer.

2. What new insight about Jesus' trial did you gain from this passage or the reference notes?

3. How does the story of Barabbas illustrate what Jesus did for you?

4. Why did Jesus go through this trial, mockery and torture when he could have used his great powers to escape? How does this make you feel?

5. CASE STUDY: Pastor Ron has been accused of sexually assaulting a member of your congregation who has a history of mental illness. The newspapers have reported the story and some of your fellow parishioners are demanding his resignation. What do you do?

TO CLOSE / 15–30 Min.

1. How did your group answer the three "Brainstorming" questions on page M19 in the center section?

2. Share your answer to one or two of the questions in APPLY.

3. If you were on trial for your spiritual life recently, how would you fare?

4. How would you like the group to pray for you?

NOTES

Summary. In Mark 14:53–65, Jesus was brought before the Sanhedrin (the Jewish high court consisting of 71 men). He was found guilty of blasphemy (defaming the character of God), a crime meriting death in the Jewish system. However, the Sanhedrin's authority was limited by the Roman government, and the Jewish leaders did not have the right to carry out capital punishment. Only Rome could do that. Therefore, the leaders brought him to Pilate, the Roman governor of the area, in hopes that he would likewise find Jesus guilty of a crime meriting death. While the trial before the Sanhedrin was conducted secretly, out of the eye of the public, the trial before Pilate was held openly in a public forum.

15:1 *Very early.* The Roman court began at daybreak. This made it necessary for the Sanhedrin to meet in an all-night session to prepare their case against Jesus. They were anxious to get a quick conviction before those loyal to Jesus could find out what was going on.

decision. While the Sanhedrin could sentence a person to death, it had no authority to actually carry out that order (see John 18:31; the incident with Stephen in Acts 7:57 appears to have been more a case of mob action than judicial process). Because of this and because of their fear of the people who supported Jesus, they needed to appeal to the Roman governor to give his approval to their decision. A Roman court would consider blasphemy merely a matter of Jewish religious scruples, not a crime requiring capital punishment. Consequently, the Sanhedrin needed to work out how to present the case to Pilate so as to ensure Jesus' death. Their decision was that when they brought Jesus to Pilate they would charge him with treason against Caesar (see Luke 23:2).

led him away. They probably took him to the palace of Herod the Great. It was here where Pilate would stay when he came to Jerusalem from his official residence in Caesarea. Pilate was probably in Jerusalem to enforce Roman authority during the great gathering of pilgrims in Jerusalem for Passover.

Pilate. Pontius Pilate was the fifth procurator of Judea. He served from A.D. 26–36. Historians of the time called him an "inflexible, merciless and obstinate" man who disliked the Jews and their customs.

15:2–5 Pilate would have been given a written deposition stating the charges against Jesus. Mark briefly describes Jesus' interrogation by Pilate. The Roman trial consisted of the accusation followed by an examination of the defendant by the magistrate. Once a ruling had been made, it was carried out immediately.

15:2 *king of the Jews.* This is how the Sanhedrin translated the Jewish title "Messiah" to Pilate. While in a sense this was an accurate rendering of the Hebrew term into Greek, this translation of the title certainly made it appear that Jesus was asserting that he, not Caesar, was the king to whom the Jews owed loyalty (see John 19:12). This would clearly be a capital offense. At this point, Pilate probably viewed Jesus as the leader of a resistance movement. There is great irony in this title. Jesus has consistently refused to be the military Messiah imagined by Jewish popular culture, and yet now he will be condemned as a guerrilla!

Yes, it is as you say. This is an enigmatic expression. Literally, it reads, "You say so" (NRSV). By this statement, Jesus accepts the title, but puts Pilate in the position to take responsibility for using it.

15:3 *accused him of many things.* Luke 23:2,5 gives a sense of the kinds of charges the authorities made against Jesus. They accused him of opposing the payment of taxes to Rome, stirring up people from Galilee and Judea to insurrection, and claiming to be the rightful king of the Jews. All of these things would be seen as a direct affront against Rome.

15:4–5 All the Gospels mention how Jesus remained silent before Pilate in the face of his charges. Seeing how his teachings had been so badly twisted in order to be used against him, there was no point in speaking. Isaiah 53:7–8 speaks of how God's servant will be silent before those who accuse him falsely. If the leaders refuse to see that his whole life is a witness against the charges being made against him, words will make no difference at this point. This scene would also be of special import to the original recipients of the Gospel, some of whom would face a situation very similar to that which Jesus faced. Here, they see how he dealt with false accusations with dignity and trust in the purposes of God.

15:6–15 Pilate realized that the Sanhedrin was not motivated by any loyalty to Rome. He also recognized that Jesus was no threat to the state and that the Sanhedrin was merely using him as a pawn to get Jesus executed. However, as John 19:12 points out, Pilate could not simply release Jesus. The

Sanhedrin had made it clear that should he do so they would spread the news to Rome that Pilate had dismissed the case of a man who claimed to be a rival king to Caesar. In an attempt to avoid this dilemma, Pilate appealed to a custom of granting amnesty to a prisoner who the masses called upon him to free. It may have been a local custom during Pilate's governorship as an attempt to win favor with the Jews. As Pilate saw a crowd gathering to make their appeal for amnesty, his plan was to get them to demand the release of Jesus. Thus, he could claim to have released Jesus because of the will of the people.

15:7 *Barabbas.* Nothing is known of Barabbas, but he was probably a prominent member of a failed revolt against Rome. The irony here is that this name means "son of the father." While rejecting the true Son of the Father, the authorities chose to free the very type of man they falsely accuse Jesus of being.

15:8 *the crowd.* Popular representations of this scene often picture this as a crowd of people composed of many of the very same pilgrims who hailed Jesus as the one "who comes in the name of the Lord" (Mark 11:9) when he entered Jerusalem a week earlier. It is as though the crowd had somehow turned against him. In fact, it is most likely that this crowd did not assemble because of Jesus at all, but came to Pilate precisely to request the release of Barabbas. It must be remembered that Jesus was arrested secretly at night, tried by the Sanhedrin in a closed door session, and brought to Pilate at dawn the next morning. His closest followers had fled. Hence, there was little time or opportunity for anyone to hear of his arrest and to gather at the palace for his trial.

15:11 The crowd, having come for the sake of Barabbas, was not to be dissuaded by Pilate. The religious authorities likewise encouraged them to demand Barabbas' release and not Jesus'.

15:15 *released Barabbas.* The death of Jesus (who is innocent) in the place of Barabbas (who is guilty) portrays the atoning sacrifice of Christ in the simplest of terms: man to man. It explains what Jesus meant in Mark 10:45 when he said that he came to "give his life as a ransom for many."

flogged. This was a terrible punishment. Soldiers would use a leather thong, into which pieces of bone and lead were woven, to lash a naked and bound prisoner. The flesh would be cut to shreds.

UNIT 12—The Crucifixion / Mark 15:22-41

The Crucifixion

²²They brought Jesus to the place called Golgotha (which means The Place of the Skull). ²³Then they offered him wine mixed with myrrh, but he did not take it. ²⁴And they crucified him. Dividing up his clothes, they cast lots to see what each would get.

²⁵It was the third hour when they crucified him. ²⁶The written notice of the charge against him read: THE KING OF THE JEWS. ²⁷They crucified two robbers with him, one on his right and one on his left.ᵃ ²⁹Those who passed by hurled insults at him, shaking their heads and saying, "So! You who are going to destroy the temple and build it in three days, ³⁰come down from the cross and save yourself!"

³¹In the same way the chief priests and the teachers of the law mocked him among themselves. "He saved others," they said, "but he can't save himself! ³²Let this Christ,ᵇ this King of Israel, come down now from the cross, that we may see and believe." Those crucified with him also heaped insults on him.

The Death of Jesus

³³At the sixth hour darkness came over the whole land until the ninth hour. ³⁴And at the ninth hour Jesus cried out in a loud voice, "Eloi, Eloi, lama sabachthani?"—which means, "My God, my God, why have you forsaken me?"ᶜ

³⁵When some of those standing near heard this, they said, "Listen, he's calling Elijah."

³⁶One man ran, filled a sponge with wine vinegar, put it on a stick, and offered it to Jesus to drink. "Now leave him alone. Let's see if Elijah comes to take him down," he said.

³⁷With a loud cry, Jesus breathed his last.

³⁸The curtain of the temple was torn in two from top to bottom. ³⁹And when the centurion, who stood there in front of Jesus, heard his cry andᵈ saw how he died, he said, "Surely this man was the Son of God!"

⁴⁰Some women were watching from a distance. Among them were Mary Magdalene, Mary the mother of James the younger and of Joses, and Salome. ⁴¹In Galilee these women had followed him and cared for his needs. Many other women who had come up with him to Jerusalem were also there.

ᵃ27 Some manuscripts *left,* ²⁸*and the scripture was fulfilled which says, "He was counted with the lawless ones"* (Isaiah 53:12)
ᵇ32 Or *Messiah*   ᶜ34 Psalm 22:1
ᵈ39 Some manuscripts do not have *heard his cry and*

READ

First Reading / First Impressions: What emotions do you feel as you read this account (choose two)?

- ❏ anger
- ❏ sorrow
- ❏ anxiety
- ❏ nothing (it's too familiar)
- ❏ shame
- ❏ gratefulness
- ❏ hope
- ❏ other:_____

Second Reading / Big Idea: Using a symbol, how would you illustrate this passage?

- ❏ a black cloud blocking the sun, representing such an ominous day
- ❏ the torn curtain of the temple, representing the way to God opened
- ❏ a sunset, representing the end of an era
- ❏ a sunrise, representing the hope of the new day to come

SEARCH

1. Jesus was crucified at the third hour. What happened between the third and sixth hour? Then what happened between the sixth and ninth hour?

Third to Sixth Hour

Sixth to Ninth Hour

2. How do you think Jesus felt about the mockery he received? What was the irony of the insult in verse 31 (see note)?

3. Why do you think Jesus felt "forsaken" by God (v. 34)?

4. What made the way Jesus died unusual (v. 37; see note)?

5. What is symbolized by the temple curtain being torn in two when Jesus died (v. 38; see note)?

6. What significant role does the confession of the centurion (v. 39) play in Mark's Gospel (see note)?

APPLY
The death of Jesus is the climax of Mark's Gospel. Having studied this account, take a few minutes to reflect on its meaning to you. In the space below, write a letter to God expressing your response to the death of Jesus. (For example: *Dear God, Your Son's death makes me feel ... It makes me want to ...*)

GROUP AGENDA

After the first part, read the Scripture out loud and divide into groups of 4. Then come back together for the third part.

TO BEGIN / 10–15 Min. (Choose 1 or 2)

1. What did you get teased about when you were growing up? How did that make you feel?

2. What is the most gut-wrenching funeral you have attended?

3. What drama or movie has done the best job of portraying the death of Christ?

TO GO DEEPER / 30 Min. (Choose 2 or 3)

1. Based on the homework assignment and study notes, what stands out to you about this passage?

2. If Jesus was the Son of God, how do you explain verse 34: "My God, my God, why have you forsaken me?" (Hint: Read Rom. 3:25–26.)

3. Why do new age religions that like to talk about the beautiful things of God skip over this?

4. What dividing walls did Jesus' death destroy?

5. When did you come to believe that Jesus died as an "atonement" for your sin?

6. Are you closer to Christ now than you were five years ago? Why do you think that is?

7. CASE STUDY: Stephanie joined the Universalist Church because of its belief in a loving God and world peace. She admires Jesus for his teaching and example, but says the idea of his dying as her "substitute" is irrational. How do you answer Stephanie?

TO CLOSE / 15–30 Min.

1. Are you planning a kickoff for starting a new small group? Have you made plans for celebrating your time together as a group?

2. Share what you wrote in the APPLY section.

3. How can the group pray for you?

NOTES

Summary. After the trial by Pilate, Jesus was once again beaten by the soldiers (Mark 15:16–20) before being taken out to be crucified. In this passage, the prophecies of his death at the hands of the authorities are fulfilled (Mark 8:31; 9:12,31; 10:33–34). Here, the Son of Man truly gives his life as a ransom for many (Mark 10:45), fulfilling God's plan (Mark 14:36). It is the death of Jesus that will unlock all the mysteries about how his mission will be accomplished and will open the way into the kingdom of God. While the death of Jesus has been the event that Mark has looked toward throughout his Gospel, when it actually happens he records it in a simple, stark way. The story of the death of Jesus is rich with allusions to Psalms 22 and 69 and Isaiah 53. These allusions and images indicate that the description in Mark is more than an actual account of the Crucifixion itself. It is a pictorial interpretation of the significance of Jesus' death as understood through the OT prophecies.

15:22 _Golgotha._ The Aramaic word for "a skull." This was probably a small, round, bare hill outside Jerusalem.

15:23 _wine mixed with myrrh._ It was a Jewish custom to offer this pain-deadening narcotic to prisoners about to be crucified (see Ps. 69:21).

15:24 _they crucified him._ Josephus, the Jewish historian, calls crucifixion "the most wretched of all ways of dying." The person to be crucified was first stripped; their hands tied or nailed to the cross-beam, which was then lifted to the upright stake already in place; then the feet were nailed in place. Typically death was a slow, agonizing process which occurred through shock, suffocation and loss of blood.

Dividing up his clothes. The clothes of the condemned person belonged to the four soldiers who carried out the crucifixion (see John 19:23–24; Ps. 22:18).

15:25 _the third hour._ This would have been about 9 a.m.

15:26 _the written notice._ The crime for which the person was being crucified was specified on a whitened board fastened above the criminal.

THE KING OF THE JEWS. By posting this sign on the cross, Pilate was simply attempting to humiliate the Jews further. The intent was to communicate that Jesus' fate would be shared by anyone else who tried to assert his authority against Rome.

15:27 *robbers.* This was a term sometimes used for Zealots, the band of fiery nationalists who were committed to the violent overthrow of Rome. While "robbery" *per se* was not a capital crime, insurrection was. Perhaps these men were involved along with Barabbas in the incident mentioned in Mark 15:7. The reference to being crucified alongside criminals is probably an allusion to Isaiah 53:12.

15:29–32 Clearly Psalm 22:6–8 is in Mark's mind here.

15:29 *You who are going to destroy the temple and build it in three days.* This claim is not made by Jesus in Mark's Gospel, but it is found in John 2:19, where it is treated as a prophecy of his death and resurrection.

15:31 *He saved others ... but he can't save himself.* Mark captures the irony of the profound truth coming from the lips of those who do not understand what they are saying (see also Mark 14:61–62; 15:2). It is precisely because Jesus is saving others that his own life is forfeited (Mark 10:45).

15:32 *Those crucified with him also heaped insults on him.* Luke recounts how one of these men stopped his abuse and professed faith in Jesus as the Messiah (Luke 23:40–43). Mark's interest is in showing the depth of the rejection and abuse Jesus encountered right up to his death.

15:33 *At the sixth hour.* This is noon.

darkness. It is disputed whether this is to be understood literally or whether it is meant as symbolic language, indicating the great significance of what was happening in terms of God's judgment. The allusion here is to Amos 8:9, where the same imagery was used to describe the "dark day" when Israel would be destroyed by the Assyrians. While there were no unusual cosmic phenomena on that day when the Assyrians invaded, for Israel it was as frightening and as destructive as if darkness had descended upon them in the middle of the day. The death of Jesus was likewise a day of judgment with profound effects for all people.

the ninth hour. This is 3 p.m.

15:34 This cry is a quote from Psalm 22:1. By echoing this cry, Jesus is identified both with the suffering of the psalmist (as he experiences unjust persecution from evil people) and with the triumph of the sufferer (as he ultimately experiences God's deliverance; see Ps. 22:19–31).

15:35 *Elijah.* The people misunderstood what Jesus said. They thought he was calling upon the ancient prophet, Elijah. According to 2 Kings 2, Elijah never died; he was taken up into heaven by angels. The expectation was that Elijah would one day reappear to proclaim the advent of God's Messiah.

15:37 *a loud cry.* This is unusual. Generally the victim of crucifixion is exhausted and unconscious at the point of death. It is almost as if Jesus voluntarily gives up his life. Perhaps what Mark mentions here is the last word in the phrase, "It is finished" (see John 19:30). This echoes the enigmatic ending of Psalm 22, which asserts that as future generations tell their children about the Lord, they will declare that "he has done it." Jesus' work of securing salvation for humanity is accomplished.

15:38 *curtain of the temple.* This curtain separated the Most Holy Place (where only the high priest could enter once a year on the Day of Atonement) from the rest of the temple. It represented the barrier which stood between the people and God. This declaration that the curtain was torn in two is Mark's way of affirming that Jesus' death has opened the way for all people to have direct access to God. The barrier has been removed because the price for sin has been fully paid. People can truly be reconciled to God. The author of Hebrews develops this imagery more fully in Hebrews 9–10.

15:39 *the Son of God.* This confession concludes the second half of Mark's Gospel. In 1:1, Mark stated that what he was writing was the Good News about Jesus the Messiah, the Son of God. The first half of the Gospel ended with the confession of Peter (a Jew) that Jesus is the Messiah (Mark 8:29); the second half ends with the confession of the centurion (a Gentile) that Jesus is the Son of God. In this context, this confession is an affirmation of the deity of Jesus.

centurion. He was the supervising officer of the soldiers who carried out the execution.

15:40 *some women.* Mark names three witnesses of the Crucifixion. Mary Magdalene was from the village of Magdala on the coast of Galilee (see Luke 8:2). The other Mary had well-known sons in the early church. Salome was the wife of Zebedee and the mother of James and John (Matt. 27:56). In contrast, all the disciples had fled.

UNIT 13—Resurrection / Great Commission / Matt. 28:1-20

The Resurrection

28 *After the Sabbath, at dawn on the first day of the week, Mary Magdalene and the other Mary went to look at the tomb.*

²There was a violent earthquake, for an angel of the Lord came down from heaven and, going to the tomb, rolled back the stone and sat on it. ³His appearance was like lightning, and his clothes were white as snow. ⁴The guards were so afraid of him that they shook and became like dead men.

⁵The angel said to the women, "Do not be afraid, for I know that you are looking for Jesus, who was crucified. ⁶He is not here; he has risen, just as he said. Come and see the place where he lay. ⁷Then go quickly and tell his disciples: 'He has risen from the dead and is going ahead of you into Galilee. There you will see him.' Now I have told you."

⁸So the women hurried away from the tomb, afraid yet filled with joy, and ran to tell his disciples. ⁹Suddenly Jesus met them. "Greetings," he said. They came to him, clasped his feet and worshiped him. ¹⁰Then Jesus said to them, "Do not be afraid. Go and tell my brothers to go to Galilee; there they will see me."

The Guards' Report

¹¹While the women were on their way, some of the guards went into the city and reported to the chief priests everything that had happened. ¹²When the chief priests had met with the elders and devised a plan, they gave the soldiers a large sum of money, ¹³telling them, "You are to say, 'His disciples came during the night and stole him away while we were asleep.' ¹⁴If this report gets to the governor, we will satisfy him and keep you out of trouble." ¹⁵So the soldiers took the money and did as they were instructed. And this story has been widely circulated among the Jews to this very day.

The Great Commission

¹⁶Then the eleven disciples went to Galilee, to the mountain where Jesus had told them to go. ¹⁷When they saw him, they worshiped him; but some doubted. ¹⁸Then Jesus came to them and said, "All authority in heaven and on earth has been given to me. ¹⁹Therefore go and make disciples of all nations, baptizing them in[a] the name of the Father and of the Son and of the Holy Spirit, ²⁰and teaching them to obey everything I have commanded you. And surely I am with you always, to the very end of the age."

[a]19 Or *into*; see Acts 8:16; 19:5; Romans 6:3; 1 Cor. 1:13; 10:2 and Gal. 3:27.

READ

First Reading / First Impressions: Which picture captures the excitement of the Resurrection for you?

- ❏ the earthquake (v. 2)
- ❏ the stone rolled away (v. 2)
- ❏ the angel's appearance (v. 3)
- ❏ the look on the guards' faces (v. 4)
- ❏ the look on the women's faces (v. 9)
- ❏ other:_____

Second Reading / Big Idea: What stands out for you as an especially important verse here? Why?

SEARCH

1. Put yourself in the place of Mary Magdalene. What are you feeling in the following verses?

> **v. 1:**
>
> **vv. 2–4:**
>
> **vv. 5–7:**
>
> **v. 8:**
>
> **vv. 9–10:**

2. Both the guards (vv. 12–15) and the disciples (vv. 18–20) receive a commission. Summarize each commission in one statement.

> **guards:**
>
> **disciples:**

3. Why would the religious authorities want to fabricate the lie that Jesus' disciples stole his body, and how believable was such an explanation (see note on v. 13)?

4. Is the Great Commission still valid today? Why?

APPLY

1. Why is it important to you that Jesus came back to life?
   - ❏ I don't know if it is important to me.
   - ❏ It's important, but I don't exactly know why.
   - ❏ Jesus is alive today and involved in my life.
   - ❏ Because Jesus passed through death, I can too!
   - ❏ It means everything he said is true.
   - ❏ All my sins are forgiven.
   - ❏ The same power is available to me.
   - ❏ other:_____

2. How has your perspective of Jesus changed during these weeks of studying his life?

3. What expectations do you think Jesus has of you in regard to the Great Commission?

4. What does it mean to you that all authority has been given to Jesus, and that he will be with you always? Write your answer in the form of a one-sentence prayer.

> **Thank you, God, that …**

61

GROUP AGENDA

After the first part, read the Scripture out loud and divide into groups of 4. Then come back together for the third part.

TO BEGIN / 10–15 Min. (Choose 1 or 2)

1. How do you like to start the day on Sunday mornings?

2. When you were a child, how did you celebrate Easter?

3. How do you feel about visiting the grave of someone you loved very much?

TO GO DEEPER / 30 Min. (Choose 2 or 3)

1. If you did the homework assignment, choose one of the questions in READ or SEARCH and share your answer.

2. How would you explain the importance of Jesus' resurrection to a non-Christian?

3. When the disciples saw Jesus in Galilee, why was doubt mingled with their worship (v. 17)? What doubts get mixed in with *your* worship?

4. What difference does the resurrection of Jesus, and your own future resurrection, make in the way you live your life today?

5. As you think about Jesus' Great Commission, what holds you back from actively passing on the Good News of Christ?

6. CASE STUDY: Alice is becoming increasingly frustrated with her church. Though doctrinally correct, the church seems preoccupied with its own programs. Alice feels convicted about Jesus' words to take the Gospel into all the world, and wants her church to reach out to and bring in people who are hurting. She expresses her frustration to you. What do you suggest?

TO CLOSE / 15–30 Min.

1. Briefly share one or two of your answers to the first three questions in APPLY.

2. What have you appreciated the most about this study and this group?

3. Have you finalized your plans for the future of your group?

4. How can the group remember you in prayer? As part of your prayer time, encourage those who would like to pray the prayer they wrote for the last question in APPLY.

NOTES

Summary. The story of Jesus ends not with his death but with his resurrection. His death brought forgiveness for the sins of the world. His resurrection brought new life to humanity. Thus the story of Jesus is bounded on both ends by great miracles. It begins with the Incarnation (Jesus comes to planet earth). It ends with the Resurrection (and Ascension) as Jesus resumes his reign as the Lord of the universe. After Jesus died on the cross, his body was removed and placed in the tomb of Joseph, a member of the Sanhedrin who had opposed the action of the council (Matt. 27:57–61). The other council members, recalling how Jesus had predicted that he would rise from the dead, asked Pilate to post a guard around the tomb so that Jesus' disciples would not be able to steal the body and claim that Jesus had indeed risen from the dead (Matt. 27:62–66). Matthew then tells the story of what happened that third day. This passage tells the story of the Resurrection and the commissioning of the apostles to be Jesus' representatives throughout the world.

28:1 *After the Sabbath, at dawn on the first day of the week.* The Sabbath was considered over at 6 p.m. on Saturday. This scene takes place early on Sunday morning.

Mary Magdalene and the other Mary. While some of the Gospels mention other women who went to the tomb, all four Gospels place Mary Magdalene in a prominent role. Mark mentions that the women brought aromatic oils to anoint the body, not so much to preserve it as to honor it (much like people today would put flowers on a grave). Clearly they did not expect Jesus to have risen from the dead, since they were shocked by what they found.

28:2 *a violent earthquake.* Earthquakes were often associated with manifestations of God's appearances on earth (Hab. 3:6).

an angel of the Lord ... rolled back the stone. A tomb like this was cut out of the side of a hill. A large, disc-shaped stone was set in a groove so that it could be fairly easily rolled down to the opening to close it off. However, once in place it would have been very difficult for people to push it back up the incline.

28:3 Popular imagination often pictures angels as rather cute, chubby babies with wings or as weak, insipid, unhappy looking characters. However, throughout the Bible, angels are consistently described as majestic, awe-inspiring beings. Angels sometimes veiled their glory so that they were not recognized immediately as supernatural beings (e.g., Judges 13:17–21). But whenever an angel appears in glory, the person or group which sees it reacts in the same way as these guards (v. 4).

lightning / white as snow. Brilliant, radiant light is often associated with appearances of God in the OT. The angel reflects the glory of God.

28:4 The earthquake, the supernatural appearance of the angel, his feat of power, and his glory overwhelmed the guards. This was something entirely foreign to their experience and they were totally overcome by fear (see also Isa. 6:5; Dan. 10:7).

28:5 *Do not be afraid.* This, too, is the standard reply of an angel to the people to whom the angel is sent (Dan. 10:12; Luke 1:13,30; 2:10). While fear is an appropriate response to the glory of God, this is a word of grace to those the Lord calls to himself.

28:6 *he has risen.* In the same way that the Gospel writers report the Crucifixion in simple, stark terms (Matt. 27:35; Mark 15:24), so, too, they describe the Resurrection in a plain, unadorned way. The phrase literally reads "he has been raised," showing that God is the one who accomplished this great act. Jesus' resurrection demonstrates that the cry of the centurion was accurate: "Surely, this man was the Son of God!" (Matt. 27:54; Mark 15:39; see also Rom. 1:4).

Come and see the place where he lay. Typically, such tombs had a large antechamber, with a small two-foot-high doorway at the back which led into the six- or seven-foot burial chamber proper. This was the tomb of a wealthy family. See Isaiah 53:9, which says the Suffering Servant would be buried with the rich. The stone was rolled away not so that the resurrected Jesus could leave the tomb (he was already gone), but so that his disciples could see that it was empty (see John 20:8).

28:7 *go / tell.* Under Jewish law, women were not considered reliable witnesses. That they were the first to know of Jesus' resurrection was somewhat of an embarrassment to the early church (see Luke 24:11,22–24), hence guaranteeing this detail is historically accurate.

his disciples. They may have abandoned Jesus, but he has not abandoned them! Mark records that

a special word was given to Peter. After his abysmal failure, Peter might have been tempted to count himself out of further discipleship.

into Galilee. Jesus said he would meet them again in Galilee (Matt. 26:32). The ministry of Jesus and the Twelve began in Galilee, and now they are directed back there to meet the risen Lord. This brings the account full circle.

28:8 *afraid yet filled with joy.* What they had experienced was radically unsettling. At the same time, the news delivered by the angel was so good they could scarcely believe it. Fear and joy were all mixed together.

28:9 *worshiped him.* This is the first mention in Matthew of people worshiping Jesus (see also v. 17). Whereas an angel rebukes John the apostle for bowing down to worship him (Rev. 22:8–9), Jesus accepts their worship. Since Jesus himself affirmed that only God should be worshiped (Matt. 4:10), this is a tacit acknowledgement of his divinity.

28:11–15 Only Matthew records this account of what the guards did after the Resurrection.

28:12 The Sanhedrin decided to try to buy off the guards so that they would not tell what had really happened.

28:13 *You are to say.* While verses 19–20 tell of Jesus' commission to his disciples, this is the Sanhedrin's commission to the guards. The disciples are motivated and encouraged in their task by the living presence of Jesus (v. 20), while the guards are motivated only by money.

His disciples came during the night and stole him away while we were asleep. This attempt at "damage control" was weak. The very reason the guards were posted was to keep the disciples from trying to steal the body and concoct a story about resurrection. For a band of frightened men to be able to elude a Roman guard, roll the tombstone uphill without waking anyone, and steal away with the body stretched the limits of believability.

28:14 *If this report gets to the governor.* For a Roman guard to fall asleep on duty was an offense meriting execution. The Sanhedrin hopes Pilate will simply not find out about what happened. However, if the story they circulate reaches his ears, they will simply bribe him to forget about punishing the Roman soldiers.

28:15 *this story has been widely circulated.* It is assumed that this Gospel was written around A.D. 80, about 50 years after this all took place. Today, the theory that Jesus' body was stolen by the disciples has been popularized by Hugh Schonfields's book, *The Passover Plot.*

28:16–20 Matthew returns to the main story as he sums up what happened when Jesus met with his disciples in Galilee.

28:16 *to the mountain.* We are not told which mountain this was. As was the case with the Transfiguration, the location of the mountain is not as significant as the theological meaning of mountains. See note on Mark 9:2 in Unit 8.

28:17 *some doubted.* So stupendous, so without precedent, is the resurrection of Jesus that right from the beginning his disciples had difficulty accepting it. When the women reported what had happened at the tomb, the Eleven said it sounded like nonsense (Luke 24:9–11). After 10 of the disciples (all but Thomas) met the resurrected Jesus and believed (Luke 24:36–49), Thomas still doubted (John 20:24–29). Here, even while worshiping the resurrected Jesus, there is still some doubt.

28:18–20 This statement is known as the Great Commission. Because all authority in heaven and earth now belongs to Jesus, he sends his disciples to spread his message everywhere with the promise that he himself is with them to the end of time.

28:18 *All authority in heaven and on earth has been given to me.* This is the meaning of the statement "Jesus is Lord." Since there is no power greater than his (Rom. 8:38–39; Phil. 2:9–11; Col. 1:15–20), there is no other loyalty to which his disciples can give their absolute allegiance.

28:19 *go and make disciples.* Literally, this is "as you are going, make disciples." The point is not so much that the apostles are to travel far and wide, but that as they go about their business (whatever that is and wherever it takes them), they are to be teaching people about Jesus and his kingdom. This is to be their pressing concern.

of all nations. The inclusive nature of Jesus' mission is crystal-clear: his kingdom includes all types of people. There are no geographic, racial, ethnic or national realms that are outside of the authority and concern of Jesus.

in the name of the Father and of the Son and of the Holy Spirit. This is a clear trinitarian formula. While the doctrine of the Trinity was not clearly articulated and defined until the third century, the roots of its teaching are clearly seen here. There is one name (or character) that defines the triune God. To be baptized "in his name" (literally "into the name") means to enter into fellowship with him.

28:20 *I am with you always.* This is the climactic promise of the new covenant. The presence of God with his people was always the goal toward which Israel looked under the old covenant. In Jesus, that presence is assured through the indwelling of Christ's Spirit (John 14:16–17).

to the very end of the age. This covers all time until the return of Christ when the new heaven and new earth will be revealed.